TWO COMIC DIALOGUES:

ION

HIPPIAS MAJOR

PLATO

TWO COMIC DIALOGUES:

ION

HIPPIAS MAJOR

Translated by
PAUL WOODRUFF

HACKETT PUBLISHING COMPANY

Copyright © 1983 by Hackett Publishing Company
Printed in the United States of America

15 14 13 12 11   5 6 7 8 9

For further information, please address
  Hackett Publishing Company, Inc.
  PO Box 44937
  Indianapolis, Indiana 46244-0937

www.hackettpublishing.com

Library of Congress Cataloging in Publication Data
Plato.
    Two Comic Dialogues
    (HPC classics series)
    Translation of: Ion and Hippias major.
    Bibliography: p.
    Contents: Ion—Hippias major.
    1. Poetics—Early works to 1800. 2. Aesthetics—
Early works to 1800. I Plato. Hippias major. English.
1983. II. Woodruff, Paul, 1943–   . III. Title.
IV. Series.
B372.A5W66   1983   184   83-269
ISBN 0-915145-76-6
ISBN 0-915145-77-4 (pbk.)

ISBN-13: 978-0-915145-76-8 (cloth)
ISBN-13: 978-0-915145-77-5 (pbk.)

The paper used in this publication meets the minimum requirements of
American National Standard for Information Sciences—Permanence of
Paper for Printed Library Materials, ANSI Z39.48–1984.

∞

For Rachel and Kate

Contents

Preface   1

Acknowledgments   3

INTRODUCTION to the ION   5

Bibliography   13

Note on the Translation   17

ION   19

Footnotes   36

INTRODUCTION to the HIPPIAS MAJOR   41

Bibliography   45

Note on the Translation   49

HIPPIAS MAJOR   51

Footnotes   80

General Index   83

Index of Ancient Works   87

Preface

Here are two of Plato's most comic dialogues. Though laced with devices from the comic stage, both treat subjects Plato took seriously. In the *Ion,* he writes in glowing metaphors of poetic inspiration, and, at the same time, he enigmatically raises grave doubts about the knowledge that was supposed in his time to come through poetry. In the *Hippias Major* he depicts Socrates' search for knowledge of what is good and beautiful, there encapsulated in the word *kalon* (translated "fine").

In the nineteenth century both dialogues were declared spurious by scholars who could not see how a work could be both comic and seriously philosophical. Our own century has been wiser, and has restored the dialogues to respectability. They are now accepted by most scholars as representative of Plato's earlier period. Together, the *Ion* and *Hippias Major* contain Plato's most important early work on poetry and beauty.

My translations are meant to be as lively as the Greek originals, yet accurate philosophically. Except where noted, I have followed Burnet's Greek text.

The introduction and notes are provided to give students and general readers the information they need to read the texts with understanding. Those who wish to go further should consult the bibliographies.

Acknowledgments

Douglass Parker and Richard McKim carefully worked through the *Ion* translation and made numerous improvements; Alexander Nehamas and Douglass Parker did the same for the *Hippias Major*. Poet Paul Foreman helped make my Homer translations in the *Ion* sound like poetry, and Betty Sue Flowers showed me how to translate the key word of that dialogue. Larry Schrenk gave me valuable help with notes and bibliographies and in many other ways. Grace Killen typed the manuscript. To all of these I am very grateful.

Introduction to the ION

THE *Ion* is one of Plato's riddles. In it he portrays Socrates (?469–399) trying to convince a reluctant Ion that poetry and related achievements come by divine inspiration. The story Plato has Socrates tell about inspiration glorifies poetry as a gift from the gods, but it reduces each poet to the role of a medium through which poems are given us. The dialogue is a major source for Plato's views on poetry and the arts. It is also a striking example of his comic technique.

AUTHENTICITY. Because the intensity of Socrates' comic attack on Ion was too much for many nineteenth-century critics, the dialogue was widely regarded as spurious. Still, the *Ion* must have been written during Plato's lifetime, for Xenophon apparently knew of the work (see below, note 21). In fact, the suspicion of forgery was aroused only by the judgment in certain quarters that the *Ion* was "unworthy of Plato." In the absence of any solid evidence against its authenticity, we should accept the *Ion* into the canon of Plato's works.*

DATE. The dramatic date of the dialogue is probably before 412 B.C., when Ephesus left its alliance with Athens (see below, note 26). The foreign officials mentioned at 541cd, however, may not have been prominent until after that date (note 25). As often happens, Plato does not allow us to assign a definite dramatic date. As to the actual date of writing, we can only speculate. The consensus of scholars makes it a fairly early work, probably written before 390 B.C.

CHARACTERS. Ion was a rhapsode from the city of Ephesus, on the coast of Asia Minor. We know nothing about him but what Plato reveals in this dialogue. Rhapsodes were professional reciters of poetry. In the beginning, they may themselves have been epic poets as

---

*For a thorough treatment of this issue, see Louis Méridier's introduction to Volume V of the Budé Series (*Platon; oeuvres complètes:* Paris, 1931), pp. 17–22.

well, but in Plato's day they were merely intermediaries between poet and audience. The poets in the repertoire of rhapsodes were Homer, Hesiod, Archilochus, Mimnermus, and Phocylides (so Athenaeus XIV.620). Rhapsodes performed at religious festivals and games, where they held forth, richly costumed and standing on elevated platforms, competing for prizes. They also performed frequently on private occasions; one of Xenophon's characters said he heard them every day (*Symposium* iii.6). Ion considers it part of his profession to explain what he recites to his audience, and in this he compares himself to the philosopher Metrodorus and the biographer Stesimbrotus, who were not considered rhapsodes (below, note 2). But interpretation (except in the sense in which an actor *interprets* his lines by delivering them in a certain way) was not part of the traditional rhapsode's profession.

Ion considered himself not only a fine actor, but an authority on Homer and on the subjects treated by Homer. This pride in his authoritative knowledge is what makes Ion a fit target for Socrates. We must remember that Homer was revered in antiquity not merely as a maker of beautiful poems, but as a source of information, particularly on military matters (see Aristophanes' *Frogs* 1032 ff., for example). Elsewhere, in the *Republic* (e.g., at 588d, ff.), Plato combats Homer's authority by direct arguments buttressed with a metaphysical theory. Here in the *Ion*, without such a theory, he must deal with the matter in a more personal and Socratic way. We know that Socrates investigated the knowledge of poets (*Apology* 22a–c); but the poets he could have known had not the authority of Homer. To attack Homer he would have to attack his representatives, the rhapsodes, of whom Ion must have presented a particularly vulnerable example. Like all of Socrates' targets, Ion is proud; and though he is no doubt good at his own trade, he is not able to make the sorts of distinctions he would need to extricate himself from Socrates' traps.

Socrates, as Plato represents him, is a man of many questions and few answers, with a mission for investigating the claims of people like Ion to expert knowledge. That is because Socrates identifies knowledge with virtue, and because he ostensibly hopes to gain by questioning those who have knowledge. He is always disappointed, not surprisingly, for his standards of knowledge are very high. Yet his disappointments pose a problem for him: how is it that the people he questions are able to carry out their work successfully? It cannot be that they do it by knowledge. Socrates usually solves the problem by attributing the success of successful people to inspiration (*Apology* 22c, *Meno* 99cd), and says no more about the matter. But in the *Ion* he says a great deal about inspiration. That is the main point of interest in the dialogue.

KNOWLEDGE (*Technē*). The pivot of Socrates' argument is the concept of *technē*—the professional knowledge of a master craftsman. A person with a *technē* has mastered a complete body of knowledge, and can do well any job that belongs to his profession. But what belongs to one profession may not belong to another: it is one thing to be a general, another to be a mathematician, and still another to be a rhapsode. To have a *technē*, moreover, is to know what in a given line of work is really good or bad, so that a doctor would be more likely than a fashionable chef to have mastered the *technē* of nutrition (*Gorgias* 463e–465d). Hence no one who measures his success merely by popular opinion, rather than by the facts, can lay claim to a *technē*, according to Socrates. This alone would suffice to discredit Ion, whose job it is to please audiences; but Socrates does not use this argument, for he wants to leave open the possibility that Ion actually speaks the truth, though without being entitled to do so by having a *technē*. Ion, Socrates argues, is inspired.

INSPIRATION. The earliest Greek poets were said to sing their songs under the influence of the divine Muses, the daughters of Zeus. Homer's great lays begin with invocations to the Muse, and when he sings of poets, he always gives the Muses their due. Demodocus, the poet of the Phaeacians, is one whom the Muse cherished, and gave "both good and evil; she destroyed his sight and gave him sweet song" (*Odyssey* 8.62–3). When the moment is right, and he has been fed, she it is who moves him to sing (8.72–3). We should remember that for a person to be aided in what he or she does by the gods is nothing special to poets in Homer's world. Success cannot come in any other way than from the gods; but this does not completely undermine human responsibility. The bard of Ithaca, Phemius, is able to say, "I am self-taught, and the god has put all sorts of tales in my mind" (*Odyssey* 22.347–8), without any sense of contradicting himself. Inspiration is neither extraordinary nor supernatural in Homer's world.

Hesiod too represents himself as an inspired poet. The Muses "breathed into me a divine voice," he says, and they gave orders that he always mention them first and last when he sang (*Theogony* 31–34). Pindar too presents himself as inspired (e.g., at *Paean* VI.6), and many other poets sing of themselves as friends, servants, or messengers of the Muses.

When Plato speaks of inspiration in poets he calls it an old story

(*Laws* 719c) and attributes it to the poets themselves (*Ion* 534a). But this is not true. What Plato says on inspiration is quite startlingly new: that when poets compose poetry they are literally out of their minds, that they are merely instruments through whom the gods speak. This idea shows up first in Plato's *Ion,* and later in the *Phaedrus* and the *Laws:*

> ... if any man comes to the gates of poetry without the madness of the Muses, persuaded that skill (*technē*) alone will make him a good poet, then shall he and his works of sanity with him be brought to nought by the poetry of madness. ... (*Phaedrus* 245a, translated by Hackforth.)

> 'Tis an old story ... that when a poet takes his seat on the Muse's tripod, his judgement takes leave of him. He is like a fountain which gives free course to the rush of its waters. (*Laws* 719c, translated by A. E. Taylor.)

He says similar things of diviners too: "No one in his right mind touches on the true inspired divinination. ... (*Timaeus* 71e); and in general, Plato chooses to liken poets to people who are frenzied or in ecstasy. The tripod in *Laws* 719c is an allusion to the Tripod at Delphi where the Pythia sat, the seer who uttered oracles in strange tongues while in an ecstatic trance. The poets are apparently like *her,* the ecstatic priestess who does not know what she is saying, and not like the more sober prophets who translate what the god says into the vernacular (cf. *Timaeus* 71e–72b). This idea, that poets are not responsible for their work and that they do not know what they are saying, is more radical than anything we find in the poetry of inspiration. It is probably a new idea with Plato.*

INSPIRATION AS MADNESS. The first thing to notice about Plato's account of inspiration is that it is literally false. If Plato were right, Ion would be in ecstasy when he recites Homer; but this he plainly is not (*Ion* 535e, 536d). Nor, as we have seen, do poets before Plato report the experience of poetic madness. Even Plato cannot believe the story: if it

---

*A late tradition attributes the idea of poetic madness to the philosopher Democritus, a generation before Plato (Diels-Kranz 68 B17–18). But this attribution is by no means certain. On the origins of the idea of poetic madness, see E. N. Tigerstedt, "*Furor Poeticus:* Poetic Inspiration in Greek Literature before Democritus and Plato," *Journal of the History of Ideas,* XXXI (1970), 163–78.

were true, the poets' songs would be as true as oracles, but Plato does not accept poetry in that light. In Books II, III, and X of the *Republic* he rejects first some and then all of the most serious Greek poetry as false. This he could not seriously do if he believed the inspiration story he himself tells.

It is no wonder that no one believes Plato's story. It is, on the face of it, false. People in ecstatic conditions are known to dance and shriek and to speak in tongues, but from a person in such a condition we do not expect articulate speech to emerge, much less poetry.

Why then does Plato have Socrates speak so forcefully in the *Ion* on behalf of an unbelievable theory of inspiration? There are a number of possibilities:

1. Plato really did want to make the theory believable, in spite of everything; he wrote the *Ion* to the greater glory of poetry. (This was the verdict of the early Renaissance, and has led to the popularity in modern times of the idea of poetic madness.)

2. Plato is here making a nasty joke on poetry, by attacking with "Aristophanic malice" its claim to inspiration. (This was the verdict of Goethe, and influenced the decision of nineteenth-century scholars to reject the dialogue as spurious.)

3. The *Ion* is part of Plato's broad critique of poetry and its disciples. It is, like the rest of that critique, mitigated by a considerable respect on Plato's part for poets. Plato could be saying to the poets, "You are wonderfully fortunate people to be so blessed by the gods, but really, you are no more in a state of knowledge about what you do than is the ecstatic Pythia." This could be a simple dismissal of the claims of poetry, or it could be an invitation to philosophers to do for poets what prophets do for the Pythia—to translate their utterances into acceptable form. (This strategy of assimilating the *Ion* to Plato's broad critique of poetry comes as close as possible to being the modern consensus.)

As is usual with Plato, we would be wrong to give a simple answer. The comic treatment of Ion is indeed Aristophanic, but it is not entirely malicious, for the language in which Socrates speaks of inspiration glows with genuine excitement. We must not forget that the poetry Plato rejected in the *Republic* was something he deeply loved.

THE ARGUMENTS. The arguments of the *Ion* are straightforward. The first (531a–536d) begins from the premise that mastery of a *technē* gives mastery of an entire body of knowledge. Ion is clever only on Homer; his cleverness is therefore not a *technē*. If not a *technē,* what is it? Socrates suggests that it is due to inspiration, and in this explanation he links Ion to the poets. They too are inspired; that is why they are limited in what they can do. The second argument (536e–end) assumes that for any *technē* there will be a well-defined professional subject matter that it will not share with other professions. Ion's subject matter is just the various subject matter of Homer himself, which ranges too widely to be known by any one profession. And the specific *technē* Ion claims to have learned best from Homer is a profession that is not his own, but belongs to commanding generals. Ion is therefore unable to identify any *technē* that he has mastered *as a rhapsode*. Here also the poets are tarred by the brush that blackens Ion, for if *he* is master of no special subject matter, then neither are they.

The second argument plays on words in an illuminating way. Ion believes that Homer's treatments of such topics as warfare are made well (*kalōs*), and Socrates is willing to concede the point. But Socrates probably means that while they are beautiful to the ear—well made in one sense of *kalōs*—they are not obviously well made in respect of truth. If Ion wished to save himself from logical disaster, he would have to distinguish between verses that are well made because they are true, and verses that are well made because they are beautiful to the ear. But Ion could never make this distinction and still cling to the idea that Homer was an authority on such matters as warfare. Whatever else this argument does, it points to the conclusion (which would have been a novelty in Plato's time) that poetry should be judged by different standards from those we use in more ordinary life—that, for example, what a general should say in a real battle is different from what a general should be made to say in a poem about a battle. If this was Plato's intention, it makes the *Ion* of prime significance in the history of literary criticism.

THE TARGET. I have taken it for granted that Plato's target in the *Ion* was poetry in general and Homer specifically, as in the *Republic*. Not all scholars agree to this. Some would have it that the *Ion* is a simple attack on Ion and his guild of rhapsodes. Others have suggested that Ion is a mask for Antisthenes, a contemporary rival of Plato. Still others have proposed to read the *Ion* as part of Plato's general attack on the sophists (of which we shall see a fine example in the *Hippias Major*).

None of these accounts of the *Ion* is persuasive. Ion himself does not deserve an attack from Plato, and neither does his guild, for the danger Plato sees in the rhapsodes lies not in *their* prestige but in that of the poets they represent. And the suggestion that Ion stands for a contemporary rival of Plato's is wholly without evidence. The idea that Ion represents sophistry is not well supported by the facts either. Those interested in pursuing these lines of interpretation should consult the works by Méridier and Tigerstedt listed in the bibliography.

On the whole, the most likely interpretation of the *Ion* is the one I have sketched in these pages. The dialogue works through the medium of a rhapsode to bring Socrates face to face with the poet he most admired, his great antagonist, Homer.

Bibliography

On inspiration and poetic madness Plato's chief work, besides the *Ion,* is the *Phaedrus.* Other relevant texts occur in the *Apology* (22c), *Meno* (99cd), *Laws* (719c), and *Timaeus* (71e–72b). On technē, see the *Hippias Minor* and the *Gorgias.*

Plato's criticism of poetry is delivered mainly in the *Republic,* Books II–III and X.

SELECT BIBLIOGRAPHY FOR THE *ION*

On the ION

Dorter, Kenneth. "The *Ion:* Plato's Characterization of Art." *The Journal of Aesthetics and Art Criticism,* XXXII (1973), 65–78.

(A useful discussion of the *Ion* in relation to Plato's wider approach to art.)

Flasher, Hellmut. *Der Dialog Ion als Zeugnis platonischer Philosophie.* (Deutsche Akademie der Wissenschaften zu Berlin, Schriften der Sektion für Altertumswissenschaft) Berlin: Akademie-Verlag, 1958.

(A controversial account of the *Ion* with a critical survey of the literature on the dialogue.)

Guthrie, W.K.C. *A History of Greek Philosophy.* Volume IV (Plato; the Man and His Dialogues: Earlier Period). Cambridge: Cambridge University Press, 1975.

(Guthrie's discussion of the *Ion,* pp. 199–212, is especially fine. The most accessible scholarly discussion of the dialogue.)

Méridier, Louis. *Platon: oeuvres complètes.* Tome V, Part I (*Ion, Menexenus, Euthydemus*). Paris: Budé Series, 1931.

(The most useful general edition; contains a fine introduction and helpful notes.)

Miller, Andrew M. *Plato's Ion.* Bryn Mawr: Bryn Mawr College, 1981.

(A helpful commentary for beginning Greek students who wish to attempt the *Ion* in the original.)

Moore, John D. "The Dating of Plato's *Ion.*" *Greek, Roman and Byzantine Studies,* 15 (1974), 421-39.

(A technical but important discussion of the problem.)

Tigerstedt, E.N. *Plato's Idea of Poetical Inspiration.* (*Commentationes Humanarum Litterarum, Societas Scientiarum Fennica,* Volume 44, Number 2.) Helsinki, 1969.

(Pp. 11–22 are a thorough treatment of the *Ion* and *Ion* scholarship, the best available.)

On Plato on Poetry and the Arts

Moravcsik, Julius and Temko, Philip, eds. *Plato on Beauty, Wisdom and the Arts.* Totowa, N.J.: Rowman and Littlefield, 1982.

(A collection of essays representing the most recent and the best scholarly work in this area.)

On Inspiration

Partee, Morriss Henry. "Inspiration in the Aesthetics of Plato." *Journal of Aesthetics and Art Criticism,* XXX (1971), 87–95.

(Partee distinguishes the inspiration of poets from other sorts of inspiration that concern Plato.)

Russell, D.A. *Criticism in Antiquity.* Berkeley: University of California Press (1981).

(C. V, pp. 69–83, is a discussion of ancient theories of inspiration.)

Tigerstedt, E.N. "*Furor Poeticus;* Poetic Inspiration in Greek Literature before Democritus and Plato." *Journal of the History of Ideas,* XXXI (1970), 163–178.

(Includes a thorough scholarly review of the literature on the problem and argues that Plato's idea of inspiration is original.)

On Technē

Irwin, Terence. *Plato's Moral Theory: The Early and Middle Dialogues.* Oxford, Clarendon Press, 1977.

(Pp. 71–77 deal with Socrates' interest in *technē* [translated as "craft" by Irwin]. His notes 39–44, pp. 297–98, survey the scholarly literature on the subject.)

Sprague, Rosamond Kent. *Plato's Philosopher King: A Study of the Theoretical Background.* Columbia, S.C.: University of South Carolina Press, 1976.

(Pp. 1–14 discuss the *Ion* in the context of a general treatment of Socrates' views on *technē.*)

Note on the Translation

In order to produce smooth intelligible English I have had to render certain words in unconventional ways.

1. *Technē*. Both stages of the argument hinge on this word, which Socrates uses for the highest sort of knowing how to do something. It is frequently translated "art," but this is misleading, for *technē* has no special connection with the fine arts. Moreover, we use "art" to cover the ability of a craftsman to do something he cannot explain how to do, but Socrates would withhold *technē* from such mysterious abilities. Other common translations for *technē* are "skill" and "craft," but neither of those things is good enough to be a *technē*. Here I have used "mastery" in the first stage of the argument and "profession" in the second. The reader should keep in mind that the same Greek word is used in both places.

2. *Hermeneus*. Usually translated "interpreter," *hermeneus* can be used of a variety of mediating roles. Here it cannot consistently mean a person who interprets in the sense of "explains," since (a) explaining a text is not a normal part of a rhapsode's profession, and (b) a rhapsode who is out of his mind (as Socrates argues Ion is) is in no position to explain anything. I have therefore translated the word as "representative." A rhapsode presents poetry as an actor presents his lines; in doing so, he does interpret them, i.e., he gives to them a certain expression. *Hermeneus* or its verbal cognate occurs at 530c3, 534e4, 535a5–9.

3. *Kalos*. In the *Hippias Major* I have translated this consistently as "fine"; but in the *Ion* I found it necessary to use a variety of renderings. Foremost among these are "lovely" and "beautiful," which allow me to preserve Socrates' guiding pun on "beautiful description." (A beautiful description may be one that is true or one that is poetical. Socrates cares only for the true; Ion is confused on the matter.) In one context, to avoid confusion, I have used "good" and "better" (538a7, 538b2).

ION

Socrates. Ion! Hello. Where have you come from to visit   530a
us this time? From your home in Ephesus?

Ion. No, no, Socrates. From Epidaurus, from the festival
of Asklepius.[1]

S. Don't tell me the Epidaurians hold a contest for
rhapsodes in honor of the god?

I. They certainly do! They do it for every sort of poetry
and music.

S. Really? Did you enter the contest? And how did it go for
you?

I. First prize, Socrates! We carried it off.   530b

S. That's good to hear. Well, let's see that we win the
games at Athens, next.

I. We'll do it, Socrates, god willing.

S. You know, Ion, many times I've envied you rhapsodes
your profession. Physically, it is always fitting for you in your
profession to be dressed up to look as beautiful as you can; and
at the same time it is necessary for you to be at work with
poets—many fine ones, and with Homer above all, who's the
best poet and the most divine—and you have to learn his   530c
thought, not just his verses! Now that is something to envy! I
mean, no one would ever get to be a good rhapsode if he didn't
understand what is meant by the poet. A rhapsode must come
to present the poet's thought to his audience; and he can't do
that beautifully unless he knows what the poet means. So this
all deserves to be envied.

I. That's true, Socrates. And that's the part of my
profession that took the most work. I think I speak more
beautifully than anyone else about Homer; neither Metrodorus   530d
of Lampsacus nor Stesimbrotus of Thasos nor Glaucon[2] nor
anyone else past or present could offer as many beautiful
thoughts about Homer as I can.

S. That's good to hear, Ion. Surely you won't begrudge me a demonstration?

I. Really, Socrates, it's worth hearing how well I've got Homer dressed up. I think I'm worthy to be crowned by the Sons of Homer[3] with a golden crown.

531a   *S.* Really, I shall make time to hear that later. Now I'd just like an answer to this: Are you so wonderfully clever about Homer alone—or also about Hesiod and Archilochus?[4]

I. No, no. Only about Homer. That's good enough, I think.

S. Is there any subject on which Homer and Hesiod both say the same things?

I. Yes, I think so. A good many.

S. Then, on those subjects, would you explain Homer's verse better and more beautifully than Hesiod's?

531b   *I.* Just the same Socrates, on those subjects, anyway, where they say the same things.

S. And how about the subjects on which they do not say the same things? Divination,[5] for example. Homer says something about it and so does Hesiod.

I. Certainly.

S. Well. Take all the places where those two poets speak of divination, both where they agree and where they don't: who would explain those better and more beautifully, you, or one of the diviners if he's good?

I. One of the diviners.

S. Suppose *you* were a diviner: if you were really able to explain the places where the two poets agree, wouldn't you also know how to explain the places where they disagree?

I. That's clear.

531c   *S.* Then what in the world is it that you're clever about in Homer but not in Hesiod and the other poets? Does Homer speak of any subjects that differ from those of *all* the other poets? Doesn't he mainly go through tales of war, and of how people deal with each other in society—good people and bad, ordinary folks and craftsmen? And of the gods, how *they* deal with each other and with men? And doesn't he recount what happens in heaven and in hell, and tell of the births of gods and

531d   heroes? Those are the subjects of Homer's poetry-making, aren't they?

I. That's true, Socrates.

S. And how about the other poets? Didn't they write on the same subjects?

I. Yes, but Socrates, they didn't do it the way Homer did.

S. How, then? Worse?

I. Much worse.

S. And Homer does it better?

I. *Really* better.

S. Well now, Ion, dear heart, when a number of people are discussing arithmetic, and one of them speaks best, I suppose *someone* will know how to pick out the good speaker.   531e

I. Yes.

S. Will it be the same person who can pick out the bad speakers, or someone else?

I. The same, of course.

S. And that will be someone who has mastered arithmetic, right?

I. Yes.

S. Well. Suppose a number of people are discussing healthy nutrition, and one of them speaks best. Will one person know that the best speaker speaks best, and another that an inferior speaker speaks worse? Or will the same man know both?

I. Obviously, the same man.

S. Who is he? What do we call him?

I. A doctor.

S. So, to sum it up, this is what we're saying: when a number of people speak on the same subject, it's always the same person who will know how to pick out good speakers and   532a bad speakers. If he doesn't know how to pick out a bad speaker, he certainly won't know a good speaker—on the same subject, anyway.

I. That's so.

S. Then it turns out that the same person is "wonderfully clever" about both speakers.

I. Yes.

S. Now *you* claim that Homer and the other poets (including Hesiod and Archilochus) speak on the same subjects, but not equally well. *He's* good, and they're inferior.

I. Yes, and it's true.

S. Now if you really do know who's speaking well, you'll   532b know that the inferior speakers are speaking worse.

I. Apparently so.

S. You're superb! So if we say that Ion is equally clever about Homer and the other poets, we'll make no mistake. Because you agree yourself that the same person will be an adequate judge of all who speak on the same subjects, and that almost all the poets *do* treat the same subjects.

I. Then how in the world do you explain what *I* do, Socrates? When someone discusses another poet I pay no attention, and I have no power to contribute anything worthwhile: I simply doze off. But let someone mention Homer and right away I'm wide awake and I'm paying attention and I have plenty to say.

S. *That*'s not hard to figure out, my friend. Anyone can tell that you are powerless to speak about Homer on the basis of knowledge or mastery. Because if your ability came by mastery, you would be able to speak about all the other poets as well. Look, there is an art of poetry as a whole, isn't there?

I. Yes.

S. And now take the whole of *any* other subject: won't it have the same discipline throughout? And this goes for every subject that can be mastered.[6] Do you need me to tell you what I mean by this, Ion?

I. Lord, yes, I do, Socrates. I love to hear you wise men talk.

S. I wish that were true, Ion. But wise? Surely you are the wise men, you rhapsodes and actors, you and the poets whose work you sing. As for me, I say nothing but the truth, as you'd expect from an ordinary man. I mean, even this question I asked you—look how commonplace and ordinary a matter it is. Anybody could understand what I meant: don't you use the same discipline throughout whenever you master the whole of a subject? Take this for discussion—painting is a subject to be mastered as a whole, isn't it?

I. Yes.

S. And there are many painters, good and bad, and there have been many in the past.

I. Certainly.

S. Have you ever known anyone who is clever at showing what's well painted and what's not in the work of Polygnotus,[7] but who's powerless to do that for other painters? Someone who dozes off when the work of other painters is displayed, and is lost, and has nothing to contribute—but when he has to

532c

532d

532e

533a

give judgment on Polygnotus or any other painter (so long as it's just *one*), he's wide awake and he's paying attention and he has plenty to say—have you ever known anyone like that?

I. Good lord no, of course not!

S. Well. Take sculpture. Have you ever known anyone who is clever at explaining which statues are well made in the case of Daedalus, son of Metion, or Epeius, son of Panopeus, or Theodorus of Samos,[8] or any other *single* sculptor, but who's lost when he's among the products of other sculptors, and he dozes off and has nothing to say? 533b

I. Good lord no. I haven't.

S. And further, it is my opinion, you've never known anyone ever—not in flute-playing, not in cithara-playing, not in singing to the cithara,[9] and not in rhapsodizing—you've never known a man who is clever at explaining Olympus or Thamyrus or Orpheus or Phemius, the rhapsode from Ithaca,[10] but who has nothing to contribute about Ion, the rhapsode from Ephesus, and cannot tell when he does his work well and when he doesn't— you've never known a man like that. 533c

I. I have nothing to say against you on that point, Socrates. But *this* I know about myself: I speak about Homer more beautifully than anybody else and I have lots to say; and everybody says I do it well. But about the other poets I do not. Now see what that means.

S. I do see, Ion, and I'm going to announce to you what I think that is. As I said earlier, that's not a subject you've mastered—speaking well about Homer; it's a divine power that moves you, as a "Magnetic" stone moves iron rings. (That's what Euripides called it; most people call it "Heracleian.")[11] This stone not only pulls those rings, if they're iron, it also puts power *in* the rings, so that they in turn can do just what the stone does—pull other rings—so that there's sometimes a very long chain of iron pieces and rings hanging from one another. And the power in all of them depends on this stone. In the same way, the Muse[12] makes some people inspired herself, and then through those who are inspired a chain of other enthusiasts is suspended. You know, none of the epic poets, if they're good, are masters of their subject; they are inspired, possessed, and that is how they utter all those beautiful poems. The same goes for lyric poets if they're good: just as the Corybantes[13] are not in their right minds when they dance, lyric poets, too, are not in their right minds when they 533d

533e

534a

make those beautiful lyrics, but as soon as they sail into harmony and rhythm they are possessed by Bacchic frenzy. Just as Bacchus worshippers[14] when they are possessed draw honey and milk from rivers, but not when they are in their right minds—the soul of a lyric poet does this too, as they say themselves. For of course poets tell us that they gather songs

534b   at honey-flowing springs, from glades and gardens of the Muses, and that they bear songs to us as bees carry honey, flying like bees. And what they say is true. For a poet is an airy thing, winged and holy, and he is not able to make poetry until he becomes inspired and goes out of his mind and his intellect is no longer in him.[15] As long as a human being has his intellect in his possession he will always lack the power to make poetry or sing prophecy. Therefore because it's not by mastery that they

534c   make poems or say many lovely things about their subjects (as you do about Homer)—but because it's by a divine gift—each poet is able to compose beautifully only that for which the Muse has aroused him: one can do dithyrambs, another encomia, one can do dance songs, another, epics, and yet another, iambics;[16] and each of them is worthless for the other types of poetry. You see, it's not mastery that enables them to speak those verses, but a divine power, since if they knew how to speak beautifully on one type of poetry by mastering the subject, they could do so for all the others also. That's why the god takes their intellect away from them when

534d   he uses them as his servants, as he does prophets and godly diviners, so that we who hear should know that *they* are not the ones who speak those verses that are of such high value, for their intellect is not in them: the god himself is the one who speaks, and he gives voice through them to us. The best evidence for this account is Tynnichus from Chalcis,[17] who never made a poem anyone would think worth mentioning, *except* for the praise-song everyone sings, almost the most beautiful lyric-poem there is, and simply, as he says himself,

534e   "an invention of the Muses." In this more than anything, then, I think, the god is showing us, so that we should be in no doubt about it, that these beautiful poems are not human, not even *from* human beings, but are divine and from gods; that poets are nothing but representatives of the gods, possessed by whoever possesses them. To show *that,* the god deliberately

535a   sang the most beautiful lyric poem through the most worthless poet. Don't you think I'm right, Ion?

I. Lord yes, *I* certainly do. Somehow you touch my soul with your words, Socrates, and I do think it's by a divine gift that good poets are able to present these poems to us from the gods.

S. And you rhapsodes in turn present what the poets say.

I. That's true too.

S. So you turn out to be representatives of representatives.

I. Quite right.

S. Hold on, Ion; tell me this. Don't keep any secrets from 535b *me.* When you recite epic poetry well and you have the most stunning effect on your spectators, either when you sing of Odysseus—how he leapt into the doorway, his identity now obvious to the suitors, and he poured out arrows at his feet—or when you sing of Achilles charging at Hector, or when you sing a pitiful episode about Andromache or Hecuba or Priam, are you at that time in your right mind, or do you get beside 535c yourself?[18] And doesn't your soul, in its enthusiasm, believe that it is present at the actions you describe, whether they're in Ithaca or in Troy or wherever the epic actually takes place?

I. What a vivid example you've given me, Socrates! I won't keep secrets from *you.* Listen, when *I* tell a sad story, my eyes are full of tears; and when I tell a story that's frightening or awful, my hair stands on end with fear and my heart jumps.

S. Well, Ion, should we say this man is in his right mind 535d at times like these: when he's at festivals or celebrations, all dressed up in fancy clothes, with golden crowns, and he weeps, though he's lost none of his finery—or when he's standing among millions of friendly people and he's frightened, though no one is undressing him or doing him any harm? Is he in his right mind then?

I. Lord no, Socrates. Not at all, to tell the truth.

S. And you know that you have the same effects on most of your spectators too, don't you?

I. I know very well that we do. I look down at them every 535e time from up on the rostrum, and they're crying and looking terrified, and as the stories are told they are filled with amazement. You see I must keep my wits and pay close attention to them: if I start them crying, *I* will laugh as I take their money, but if *they* laugh, I shall cry at having lost money.

S. And you know that this spectator is the last of the rings, don't you—the ones that I said take their power from each other by virtue of the Heracleian stone [the magnet]? The

536a middle ring is you, the rhapsode or actor, and the first one is the poet himself. The god pulls people's souls through all these wherever he wants, looping the power down from one to another. And just as if it hung from that stone, there's an enormous chain of choral dancers and dance teachers and assistant teachers hanging off to the sides of the rings that are suspended from the Muse. One poet is attached to one Muse,

536b another to another (we say he is "possessed," and that's near enough, for he is *held*). From these first rings, from the poets, *they* are attached in their turn and inspired, some from one poet, some from another: some from Orpheus, some from Musaeus,[19] and many are possessed and held from Homer. You are one of *them,* Ion, and you are possessed from Homer. And when anyone sings the work of another poet, you're asleep and you're lost about what to say; but when any song of that poet is sounded, you are immediately awake, your soul is

536c dancing, and you have plenty to say. You see it's not because you're a master of knowledge about Homer that you can say what you say, but because of a divine gift, because you are possessed. That's how it is with the Corybantes, who have sharp ears only for the specific song that belongs to whatever god possesses them; they have plenty of words and movements to go with *that* song; but they are quite lost if the music is different. That's how it is with you, Ion: when anyone mentions Homer, you have plenty to say, but if he mentions the others

536d you are lost; and the explanation of this, for which you ask me—why it is that you have plenty to say about Homer but not about the others—is that it's not mastering the subject, but a divine gift, that makes you a wonderful singer of Homer's praises.

I. You're a good speaker, Socrates. Still, I would be amazed if you could speak well enough to convince me that I am possessed or crazed when I praise Homer. I don't believe you'd think so if you heard me speaking on Homer.

536e *S.* And I really do want to hear you, but not before you answer me this: on which of Homer's subjects do you speak well? I don't suppose you speak well on *all* of them.

I. I do, Socrates, believe me, on every single one!

S. Surely not on those subjects you happen to know nothing about, even if Homer does speak of them.

I. And these subjects Homer speaks of, but I don't know about—what are they?

S. But doesn't Homer speak about professional subjects   537a
in many places, and say a great deal? Chariot driving, for
example. I'll show you, if I can remember the lines.
I. No, I'll recite them. I *do* remember.
S. Then tell me what Nestor says to his son Antilochus,
when he advises him to take care at the turning post in the horse
race they held for Patroclus's funeral.
I. "Lean," he says,

> Lean yourself over on the smooth-planed chariot
> Just to the left of the pair. Then the horse on the   537b
>   right—
> Goad him, shout him on, easing the reins with your
>   hands.
> At the post let your horse on the left stick tight to
>   the turn
> So you seem to come right to the edge, with the hub
> Of your welded wheel. But escape cropping the
>   stone . . .[20]

S. That's enough. Who would know better, Ion, whether   537c
Homer speaks correctly or not in these particular verses—
a doctor or a charioteer?
I. A charioteer, of course.
S. Is that because he is a master of that profession, or for
some other reason?
I. No. It's because he's a master of it.
S. Then to each profession a god has granted the ability to
know a certain function. I mean, the things navigation teaches
us—we won't learn them from medicine as well, will we?
I. Of course not.
S. And the things medicine teaches us we won't learn from
architecture.
I. Of course not.   537d
S. And so it is for every other profession: what we learn by
mastering one profession we won't learn by mastering another,
right? But first, answer me this. Do you agree that there are
different professions—that one is different from another?
I. Yes.
S. And is this how you determine which ones are different?
When *I* find that the knowledge [involved in one case] deals
with different subjects from the knowledge [in another case],

537e then I claim that one is a different profession from the other. Is that what you do?

    I. Yes.

    S. I mean if there is some knowledge of the same subjects, then why should we say there are two different professions?— Especially when each of them would allow us to know the same subjects! Take these fingers: I know there are five of them, and you know the same thing about them that I do. Now suppose I asked you whether it's the same profession—arithmetic—that teaches you and me the same things, or whether it's two different ones. Of course you'd say it's the same one.

    I. Yes.

538a   *S*. Then tell me now what I was going to ask you earlier. Do you think it's the same way for every profession—the same profession must teach the same subjects, and a different profession, if it *is* different, must teach not the same subjects, but different ones?

    I. That's how I think it is, Socrates.

    S. Then a person who has not mastered a given profession will not be able to be a good judge of the things which belong to that profession, whether they are things said or things done.

538b   *I*. That's true.

    S. Then who will know better whether or not Homer speaks beautifully and well in the lines you quoted? You, or a charioteer?

    I. A charioteer.

    S. That's because you're a rhapsode, of course, and not a charioteer.

    I. Yes.

    S. And the rhapsode's profession is different from the charioteer's.

    I. Yes.

    S. If it's different, then its knowledge is of different subjects also.

    I. Yes.

    S. Then what about the time Homer tells how Hekamede, 538c Nestor's woman, gave barley-medicine to Machaon to drink? He says something like this—

> Over wine of Pramnos she grated goat's milk cheese
> With a brazen grater.... And onion relish for the
> drink . . .[21]

Is Homer right or not: would a fine diagnosis here come from a
doctor's profession or a rhapsode's?

I. A doctor's.

S. And what about the time Homer says:

> Leaden she plunged to the floor of the sea like a   538d
> weight
> That is fixed to a field cow's horn. Given to the hunt
> It goes among ravenous fish, carrying death.[22]

Should we say it's for a fisherman's profession or a rhapsode's
to tell whether or not he describes this beautifully and well?

I. That's obvious, Socrates. It's for a fisherman's.

S. All right, look. Suppose you were the one asking
questions, and you asked me, "Socrates, since you're finding   538e
out which passages belong to each of the professions Homer
treats—which are the passages that each profession should
judge—come tell me this: which are the passages that belong to
a diviner and to divination, passages he should be able to judge
as to whether they're well or badly composed?" Look how
easily I can give you a true answer. Often, in the *Odyssey*, he
says things like what Theoklymenus says—the prophet of the
sons of Melampus:

> Are you mad? What evil is this that's upon you? Night   539a
> Has enshrouded your hands, your faces, and down to
> your knees.
> Wailing spreads like fire, tears wash your cheeks.
> Ghosts fill the dooryard, ghosts fill the hall, they rush
> To the black gate of hell, they drop below darkness.
> Sunlight
> Has died from a sky run over with evil mist.[23]   539b

And often in the *Iliad*, as in the battle at the wall. There he says:

> There came to them a bird as they hungered to cross
> over.
> An eagle, a high-flier, circled the army's left
> With a blood-red serpent carried in its talons,   539c
> a monster,
> Alive, still breathing, it had not yet forgotten its war-
> lust,

For it struck its captor on the breast, by the neck;
It was writhing back, but the eagle shot it ground-
wards
In agony of pain, and dropped it in the midst of the
throng,

539d
Then itself, with a scream, soared on a breath of
the wind.[24]

I shall say that these passages and those like them belong to a
diviner. They are for him to examine and judge.

I. That's a true answer, Socrates.

S. Well, *your* answers are true, too, Ion. Now *you* tell
me—just as I picked out for you, from the *Odyssey* and the
Iliad, passages that belong to a diviner and ones that belong to

539e
a doctor and ones that belong to a fisherman—in the same way,
Ion, since you have more experience with Homer's work than I
do, you pick out for me the passages that belong to the
rhapsode and to his profession, the passages a rhapsode should
be able to examine and to judge better than anyone else.

I. My answer, Socrates, is "all of them."

S. That's not *your* answer, Ion. Not "all of them." Or are
you really so forgetful? But no, it would not befit a *rhapsode* to
be forgetful.

540a
I. What do you think I'm forgetting?

S. Don't you remember you said that a rhapsode's
profession is different from a charioteer's?

I. I remember.

S. And didn't you agree that because they are different
they will know different subjects?

I. Yes.

S. So a rhapsode's profession, on *your* view, will not know
everything, and neither will a rhapsode.

I. But things like that are exceptions, Socrates.

540b
S. By "things like that" you mean that almost all the
subjects of the other professions are exceptions, don't you? But
then what sort of thing *will* a rhapsode know, if not everything?

I. My opinion, anyhow, is that he'll know what it's fitting
for a man or a woman to say—or for a slave or a freeman, or for
a follower or a leader.

S. So—what should a leader say when he's at sea and his
ship is hit by a storm—do you mean a rhapsode will know
better than a navigator?

I. No, no. A navigator will know *that.*

S. And when he's in charge of a sick man, what should   540c
a leader say—will a rhapsode know better than a doctor?

I. Not that, either.

S. But he *will* know what a slave should say. Is that what
you mean?

I. Yes.

S. For example, what should a slave who's a cowherd say
to calm down his cattle when they're going wild—will a
rhapsode know what a cowherd does not?

I. Certainly not.

S. And what a woman who spins yarn should say about
working with wool?   540d

I. No.

S. And what a man should say, if he's a general, to
encourage his troops?

I. Yes! That's the sort of thing a rhapsode will know.

S. What? Is a rhapsode's profession the same as a
general's?

I. Well, *I* certainly would know what a general should say.

S. Perhaps that's because you're also a general by
profession, Ion. I mean, if you were somehow both a horseman
and a cithara-player at the same time, you would know
good riders from bad. But suppose I asked you: "Which   540e
profession teaches you good horsemanship—the one that
makes you a horseman, or the one that makes you a cithara-
player?"

I. The horseman, I'd say.

S. Then if you also knew good cithara-players from bad,
the profession that taught you *that* would be the one which
made you a cithara-player, not the one that made you a
horseman. Wouldn't you agree?

I. Yes.

S. Now, since you know the business of a general, do you
know this by being a general or by being a good rhapsode?

I. I don't think there's any difference.

S. What? Are you saying there's no difference? On your   541a
view is there one profession for rhapsodes and generals, or
two?

I. One, I think.

S. So anyone who is a good rhapsode turns out to be a
good general too.

I. Certainly, Socrates.

S. It also follows that anyone who turns out to be a good general is a good rhapsode too.

I. No. This time I don't agree.

S. But you do agree to this: anyone who is a good rhapsode
541b is a good general too.

I. I quite agree.

S. And aren't you the best rhapsode in Greece?

I. By far, Socrates.

S. Are you also a general, Ion? Are you the best in Greece?

I. Certainly, Socrates. That, too, I learned from Homer's poetry.

S. Then why in heaven's name, Ion, when you're both the best general *and* the best rhapsode in Greece, do you go around the country giving rhapsodies but not commanding troops? Do
541c you think Greece really needs a rhapsode who is crowned with a golden crown? And does not need a general?

I. Socrates, *my* city is governed and commanded by you [by Athens]; we don't need a general. Besides, neither your city nor Sparta would choose me for a general. You think you're good enough for that yourselves.

S. Ion, you're superb. Don't you know Apollodorus of Cyzike?

I. What does *he* do?

S. He's a foreigner who has often been chosen by Athens
541d to be their general. And Phanosthenes of Andros and Herakleides of Clazomenae[25]—they're also foreigners; they've demonstrated that they are worth noticing, and Athens appoints them to be generals or other sorts of officials. And do you think that *this* city, that makes such appointments, would not select Ion of Ephesus and honor him, if they thought he was worth noticing? Why? Aren't you people from Ephesus
541e Athenians of long standing? And isn't Ephesus a city that is second to none?[26]

But *you,* Ion, you're doing me wrong, if what you say is true that what enables you to praise Homer is knowledge or mastery of a profession. You assured me that you knew many lovely things about Homer, you promised to give a demonstration; but you're cheating me, you're a long way from giving a demonstration. You aren't even willing to tell me what it is that you're so wonderfully clever *about,* though I've been begging you for ages. Really, you're just like Proteus,[27] you twist up and

down and take many different shapes, till finally you've 542a
escaped me altogether by turning yourself into a general, so as
to avoid proving how wonderfully wise you are about Homer.

If you're really a master of your subject, and if, as I said
earlier, you're cheating me of the demonstration you promised
about Homer, then you're doing me wrong. But if you're not a
master of your subject, if you're possessed by a divine gift from
Homer, so that you make many lovely speeches about the poet
without knowing anything—as *I* said about you—then you're
not doing me wrong. So choose, how do you want us to think
of you—as a *man* who does wrong, or as someone *divine*?

I. There's a great difference, Socrates. It's much lovelier 542b
to be thought divine.

S. Then *that* is how we think of you, Ion, the lovelier way:
it's as someone divine, and not as master of a profession, that
you are a singer of Homer's praises.

Footnotes to the *ION*

1. Epidaurus lies across the Saronic Gulf from Athens. It was famous as a center for the healing cult of Asklepius, in whose honor a festival was held every four years. Competitive performances by rhapsodes were regular features of such festivals. In Athens, at the Panathenaia, recitations of rhapsodes were governed by laws dating at least to the beginning of the fifth century (pseudo-Plato, *Hipparchus* 228b). On rhapsodes, see p. 5–6.

2. Metrodorus of Lampsacus, a student of Anaxagoras in the fifth century B.C., was known for his allegorical interpretations, in which he gave naturalistic accounts of both gods and heroes. (See Section 61 of Hermann Diels, *Die Fragmente der Vorsokratiker,* 6th ed. rev. Walther Kranz, Berlin, 1952.) Stesimbrotus interpreted Homer (but not, apparently allegorically). His understanding of Homer is contrasted with that of the rhapsodes in Xenophon's *Symposium* iii.6. Little is known about Glaucon: he may be the figure mentioned by Aristotle at *Poetics* 1461B1, or the one in his *Rhetoric* 1403B26. None of the three was known as a rhapsode.

3. The sons of Homer were a guild of rhapsodes who originally claimed to be descendants of Homer.

4. Hesiod was the author of *Works and Days* and the *Theogony*. In early antiquity he was considered a contemporary of Homer, but he is now thought to have lived somewhat later. Archilochus was a writer of iambic poems and elegies of the eighth or seventh centuries B.C.
   Rhapsodes were not confined to reciting Homer. They gave recitations from Homer, Hesiod, Archilochus, Mimnermus, and Phocylides (Athenaeus XIV.620C, on the authority of Chamaeleon, a Peripatetic of the fourth or third century B.C.).

5. Divination was the art of interpreting portents. See 539a–d below for Homeric examples.

6. The precise sense of the Greek here is not clear. The general idea is that there is one discipline (*tropos tēs skepseōs*) for each technē.

7. Polygnotus was a well-known painter who came from Thasos to Athens and flourished there in the mid-fifth century B.C.

8. Daedalus was praised in myth as an inventor of lifelike statues for King Minos of Crete. Epeius was the legendary maker of the wooden horse that deceived the Trojans (*Odyssey* 8.493). Theodorus was an inventor and artist who flourished on Samos in the mid-sixth century B.C.

9. The cithara was a lyre-like instrument with a wooden sound-box and strings of equal length, which were plucked, usually to accompany a song.

10. Olympus was the legendary inventor of flute music. Thamyrus was a legendary Thracian cithara-player. Orpheus was a singer and lyre-player celebrated in myth. Phemius was the poet who was forced to sing for the suitors of Penelope (*Odyssey* 1.154 and 22.330).

11. Natural magnets apparently came from places called *Magnesia* and *Heracleia* in Caria in Asia Minor, and were called after those places. The reference to Euripides is Fragment 571 (Nauck) from the play *Oeneus*.

12. The Muses, who were daughters of Zeus, gave to poets gifts of memory and poetic composition. The gardens of the Muses Socrates mentions (534b1) may be an allusion to Pindar (*Olympian Ode* IX, 26-27). The analogy with bees may be drawn from Aristophanes (*Birds* 748–51). On inspiration, see above, p. 7-9.

13. The Corybantes were priests of the mother-goddess Cybele, whom they worshipped with wild music and dance.

14. Bacchus worshippers apparently danced themselves into a frenzy in which they found streams flowing with honey and milk (Euripides, *Bacchae* 708–11). For the association of poetry with milk and honey, see Pindar, *Nemean Ode* III, 77–78.

15. This is a favorite theme of Plato's. Cf. *Phaedrus* 245a and *Laws* 719c. It is not, however, a theme of the poets themselves. Though poets before Plato wrote of inspiration, they never treated it as a species of madness (see above, p. 8).

16. A *dithyramb* was a poem written to be sung by a chorus in honor of Dionysus. An *encomium* is a poem written in praise of someone, usually an athletic victor. A *dance song* (*hyporchēma*) is a form of lyric poetry for a

chorus. *Iambic poetry* was usually satirical.

Socrates is wrong on the main point. Well-known poets did compose in more than one genre. Pindar, for example, wrote in three of the forms Socrates mentions (dithyramb, encomium, and dance song).

17. Tynnichus is otherwise unknown, except that he was admired by Aeschylus (Porphyry, *De Abstinentia* 2.18).

18. Odysseus leaps to the threshhold at *Odyssey* 22.1, and reveals his identity later, at line 35. Achilles attacks Hector at *Iliad* 22.312 and following. Pitiful scenes involving Andromache occur at *Iliad* 6.370–502, 22.437–515, and 24.723–46; Hecuba at 22.79–89, 22.405, 22.430–36, and 24.747–60; and Priam at 22.33–78, 22.408–28, and 24.160–717.

19. Musaeus is, like Orpheus, a mythical singer.

20. *Iliad* 23.335–40. Xenophon uses the passage to similar effect in his *Symposium* iv.6.

21. *Iliad* 11.639—40 with 630. The drink refreshes both the wounded man, Machaon, and Nestor, who had brought him in. Pramnian wine was a proverbially healthy wine, but even the ancients were uncertain where Pramnos (or possibly Pramne) was. The passage is used similarly in Xenophon's *Symposium* iv.7, where Xenophon apparently alludes to the *Ion*.

22. *Iliad* 20.80–82. When Achilles persists in mistreating the body of Hector, Zeus sends his messenger Iris plunging down into the sea to summon Achilles' mother, Thetis. She will soften his heart.

The horn is probably used to shield the fish-line against the bites of the fish (so Plutarch, *The Cleverness of Animals* 977, following Aristarchus).

23. *Odyssey* 20.351–57; line 354 is omitted by Plato. Penelope's suitors have treated a beggar with contempt, not knowing that he is the hero who will destroy them. Now they have gone into fits of uncontrollable laughter at Telemachus. At this point, Theoklymenus sees their bloody future. Melampus, his ancestor, was a legendary seer; the sons of Melampus were a family of prophets.

The first word, *daimonioi*, does not occur in Homer's manuscripts, which have instead *a deiloi* ("O miserable wretches!"). *Daimonioi* is used in a variety of ways, but always suggests the presence of a divine force in the people addressed. Here Plato no doubt intends us to remember that poets are supposed to be beneficiaries of a divine presence.

24. *Iliad* 12.200–207. The Trojan force is eager to cross a ditch and attack the wall that guards the Achaean shipping. Poulydamas interprets the portent

correctly as bad news for the Trojans, but Hector does not believe in such things. Later, Hector does accept the advice of Poulydamas, agreeing with him that different men are given different abilities by the gods: one man is made a soldier, another receives the gift of wisdom (*Iliad* 13.729–33). Plato must have had this passage too in mind.

25. Phanosthenes is mentioned by Xenophon as active in a campaign of 408/7 B.C. Herakleides is mentioned in Pseudo-Aristotle, *The Constitution of Athens,* as playing the part of a citizen just after the restoration of democracy in Athens (403 B.C.). The *Ion's* reference to Herakleides is possibly anachronistic, if the dramatic date of the *Ion* is before 412 B.C. But see John D. Moore, "The Dating of Plato's *Ion,*" *Greek, Roman, and Byzantine Studies,* 15 (1974), 421–439.

Apollodorus is unknown, unless, as is unlikely, he is identical with the contemporary of Philip mentioned by Pausanius (I.29.10). If so, the *Ion* could not be Plato's work.

26. In legend, Ephesus was founded by a prince of Athens and was therefore, in a sense, Athenian. Ephesus was a prominent Ionian city on the coast of Asia Minor. It was allied with Athens until it revolted (probably in 412 B.C.).

27. Proteus was a servant of Poseidon. He had the power to take whatever shape he wanted in order to avoid answering questions (*Odyssey* 4.385 ff.). Cf. *Euthyphro,* 15d.

Introduction to the HIPPIAS MAJOR

TWO DIALOGUES of Socrates with Hippias come down to us under Plato's name. The *Hippias Major*, the longer of the two, is distinguished from other Platonic works by its richly comic and unusual vocabulary, and by its startling use of ridicule against Socrates' adversary. This aroused a suspicion in scholarly circles during the nineteenth century that the *Hippias Major* was not the work of Plato. Those who thought Plato would not have written two *Hippias* dialogues therefore chose the *Major* to strike from the canon. That has been a great loss, for the *Hippias Major* is likely to be authentic. It is rewarding as a uniquely comic dialogue, an intriguing piece of philosophy, and a clue to Plato's development.

AUTHENTICITY. Since the *Hippias Major* first came under suspicion, debate on its authenticity has flourished, overshadowing the many interesting features of the work itself. Those who would reject the work deemed it unworthy of Plato and were surprised by its unusual vocabulary. Defenders for the most part found the dialogue splendidly Platonic. Both sides are still at it. The issue depends too much on taste—and on taste in the shadowy realm of humor, at that—to be definitely resolved. Both sides, however, agree to date the *Hippias Major* during Plato's lifetime, and both set it apart from the general ruck of dialogues that are certainly spurious. No compelling arguments have been advanced against the *Hippias Major*. We should, therefore, accept it as genuine.*

CHARACTERS. Hippias was a traveling teacher of public speaking and various other subjects, including mathematics, astronomy, geometry, euphony, mnemonics, history, and ethics. He would give displays of oratory (or whatever else was wanted) for a substantial fee, which he

---

*For a thorough discussion of this issue, see Paul Woodruff, *Plato: Hippias Major* (Indianapolis, 1982), Chapter 1.

thought he deserved. He was in his opinion especially qualified to enhance the virtues of his paying students. In Plato's eyes that made him a sophist; and though so far as we know Hippias taught nothing morally offensive, he was himself a moral offense to Plato, somehow making it worth Plato's while a half-generation later to lambaste him through the literary person of Socrates. The ridicule is personal, for Hippias' defect was not in his beliefs (if he had any to pin down) so much as in his personality. He was the most versatile of sophists. He could teach anything, and be counted on to tell an audience what it wanted to hear. This flexibility, coming as it did with a promise of moral instruction, was morally alarming. It alarmed Plato enough to provoke him into writing not only the two Hippias dialogues, but numerous attacks on nameless sophists for their versatility, a despised quality which Hippias exemplified.

The *Hippias Major* shows Socrates mercilessly laying bare the empty core under Hippias' multifaceted veneer. He is the annoying and fascinating Socrates of the *Apology* and dialogues of search. He has a little (an important little) in common with Xenophon's Socrates. How accurate a portrait he is of the man who hooked Plato on philosophy no one can definitely say. He is interesting enough, at any rate, to be the historical Socrates. But he is connected in the *Hippias Major* with the beginnings of Plato's theory of Forms, and that theory, according to consensus, is not Socratic.

SUBJECT. Plato's subject is as alarmingly slippery as Hippias himself. It is the important thing Socrates' other objects of search have in common: the *kalon*. Variously translated "beautiful," "noble," "admirable," and "fine," *kalon* is a general term of commendation. The virtues Socrates wants to know about elsewhere are each of them *kalon*. So are the lovely boys and young men with whom he spends his days. So are sound laws and good habits, fast horses, and fierce fighting birds. So are true sentences and morally improving speeches. And so, surprisingly, is ugly old Socrates himself.

When the fashion was to translate *kalon* "beautiful," the *Hippias Major* was diminished to a disappointing treatise in aesthetics. Understood more broadly, with "fine" for *kalon* (as I translate it), the dialogue is an interesting inquiry into the foundation of all sorts of value judgments.

The slipperiness on which Socrates is trying to find ground for a firm stand is the liability of words like "fine," "good," and "large" to take on apparently different meanings in different contexts. A fine soldier may not have the qualities of a fine man, any more than a large diamond has the size of a large rock. Hippias seems content to slide with the usage of the word, but Socrates is not. Socrates wants to know the one nature that the fine is in every fine thing. Hippias does not want to know anything of the sort. He thinks he already knows how to get by, come what may, by making a crowd laugh at a person who asks questions, for example. Neither man has any part in the other's enterprise, so the contest that emerges is like what would happen if two skilled persons tried to play "Go" and Checkers against each other on the same board, using the same pieces, at the same time.

PRELIMINARY SKIRMISH. Socrates interrogates Hippias on his career—his earnings, his high opinion of himself, the subjects he teaches. Sparta, it turns out, refuses to admit Hippias as a teacher. His credentials in question, Hippias invites Socrates to hear and judge a speech Hippias gave in Sparta about what practices are fine training for young men. This reminds Socrates that the last time he tried to evaluate speeches as fine or foul, he was interrupted by someone asking him how he knew what sorts of things were fine or foul. Socrates still does not know how to answer him. Will Hippias help?

THE ARGUMENT. Through the undeceiving mask of an unnamed Questioner, Socrates asks what the fine is—what it is to be fine, or what it is that makes things fine. After showing how Hippias' three tries are all failures, he initiates a line of answers himself and drives it to an impasse. The fine turns out to be an elusive quarry. "What's fine is hard," says Socrates at the end, and that lesson appears to be the meager fruit of the dialogue. But that is neither meager nor the only accomplishment of the *Hippias Major*.

Quick learner that he is, Hippias had thought the fine would be an easy subject, like every subject for him. That was what was the matter with Hippias, that he took difficult matters to be trifles. And that, if Socrates is right in his high standards for definition, is the matter with a great many people. Showing the elusiveness of the fine, then, is of considerable importance for Socrates.

The *Hippias Major* is more than an exposure of Hippias and his overconfident kind, however. Its argument illustrates a conception of definition that was new in its time and is interesting in any time. Although so far as we know Socrates had no general theory of definition, he is clear in the *Hippias Major* about what conditions a definition of the fine should satisfy. These requirements for definition carry with them presuppositions about the nature of the fine. If the fine is to be definable by Socrates' rules, then it must turn out to be of a certain sort: it must be one and the same in every fine thing; it must always be fine, and it must be what makes fine things fine. To know such things about the fine is to know a great deal about it.

With these presuppositions comes the ghost of an ontology, the early beginnings of Plato's theory of Forms. That is what has made the *Hippias Major* important to recent scholarship on Plato's development. Socrates supposes that the fine is a form and that it is *something,* an unchanging nature. He does not go beyond this to ask how such natures fit into a general ontological theory; nor does he state or presuppose the most distinctive doctrines of the theory of Forms. That theory, nevertheless, is a natural development of the sort of thing Socrates says about the fine in the *Hippias Major.*

There is still another sort of belief about the fine that we may assign to Socrates, but more speculatively. He seems to have held that the fine is both good and beneficial, but not that it is defined as either *the* good or *the* beneficial. When Socrates knows what the fine is, he will probably know as well what both of those things are. But that is just what Socrates does not know. His ignorance is hard for him, but he is prepared to make the best of it.

On that note the dialogue ends. Hippias has learned nothing but to avoid Socrates; Socrates has only learned again how difficult a subject he has undertaken. And the reader—what should he learn? Socrates' lesson, at least, but also much about definition and something even about the fine itself.

DATE. The dramatic date for Socrates' discussion with Hippias is probably some time between 421 and 416 B.C., during the Peace of Nicias. The dialogue was certainly written during Plato's lifetime, most likely fairly early in his career, after the *Euthyphro* and before the *Phaedo,* around 390 B.C. or in the 380's.

Bibliography

For Socrates' unconventional ideas about the fine (*kalon:* fine, beautiful admirable, noble), see, for example, *Charmides* 154de and *Gorgias* 474d–475e. With these, compare Xenophon's *Symposium* v.

For more fully developed theories about *kalon* in Plato, see *Phaedo* 100cd, *Republic* 479ab, *Symposium* 210a–212a, and *Phaedrus* 250d–256e. In each case, you will need to read the wider context in order to understand the passage cited.

Other dialogues that should be compared with the *Hippias Major* are the *Euthyphro,* the *Laches,* the *Charmides,* and Book I of the *Republic.* In these dialogues Socrates is shown seeking definitions of piety, courage, temperance or sound-mindedness, and justice. His methods are similar to those he follows in the *Hippias Major.*

SELECT BIBLIOGRAPHY FOR THE *HIPPIAS MAJOR*

On the HIPPIAS MAJOR

Malcolm, John. "On the Place of the *Hippias Major* in the Development of Plato's Thought." *Archiv für Geschichte der Philosophie,* 50 (1968), 189–95.

Tarrant, Dorothy. *The Hippias Major Attributed to Plato: with Introductory Essays and Commentary.* Cambridge: Cambridge University Press, 1928. Repr. New York: Arno Press, 1973.

(A useful commentary on the Greek text, with an introduction containing an argument against authenticity.)

Woodruff, Paul. *Plato: Hippias Major.* Indianapolis: Hackett Publishing Company, 1982.

(In addition to the translation reprinted in the present book, this includes a thorough commentary and an essay on the literary and philosophical interpretation of the dialogue.)

On the Sophists and Socrates

Guthrie, W.K.C. *A History of Greek Philosophy.* vol. III: *The Fifth-Century Enlightenment.* Cambridge: Cambridge University Press, 1969. Repr. in two volumes (*The Sophists.* Cambridge: Cambridge University Press, 1971 and *Socrates.* Cambridge: Cambridge University Press, 1971).

(A fine introduction to the subject, this is especially helpful with bibliography.)

Irwin, Terence. *Plato's Moral Theory: The Early and Middle Dialogues.* Oxford: Clarendon Press, 1977.

(Includes an important and controversial study of ethical doctrines attributed to Socrates.)

Santas, Gerasimos Xenophon. *Socrates: Philosophy in Plato's Early Dialogues.* London: Routledge & Kegan Paul, 1979.

(A thorough analysis of the arguments made and positions taken by Socrates in Plato's earlier dialogues.)

Vlastos, Gregory. *The Philosophy of Socrates: A Collection of Critical Essays.* (Editor) Garden City, New York: Anchor, 1971.

(A collection of essays. Especially noteworthy for our purposes is Vlastos' "Introduction: The Paradox of Socrates" and Lacey's "Our Knowledge of Socrates.")

On Plato's Theory of Forms

Allen, R.E. *Plato's 'Euthyphro' and the Earlier Theory of Forms.* New York: Humanities Press, 1970.

Rist, J.M. "Plato's 'Earlier Theory of Forms'." *Phoenix,* 29 (1975), 336–57.

(A critical review of Allen's theory.)

Ross, W.D. *Plato's Theory of Ideas.* Oxford: Clarendon Press, 1951.

(Still the best general study of the theory.)

Wedberg, A. "The Theory of Ideas." in Gregory Vlastos ed. *Plato: A Collection of Critical Essays.* vol. I: *Metaphysics and Epistemology.* Garden City, New York: Anchor, 1971. pp. 28–52.

Note on the Translation

Much of the dialogue's argument hangs on equivocation or other word play. To carry this into English I have adhered strictly to one translation for each Greek word that is played on. The result is unusual English in a few contexts.

Examples:

kalos is "fine" throughout, though some contexts taken alone would call for "beautiful" or "good." Its opposite, *aischros,* is "foul" throughout.

phainesthai is "to be seen." When it occurs, as often in the *Hippias Major,* alone with an adjective, it is ambiguous between "is plainly" (with a participle understood) and "is thought to be" (with an infinitive understood).

dunatos is "able," though one context calls for "powerful."

I have otherwise tried to capture Plato's conversational style, except in those passages in which he abandons it himself. Often in the *Hippias Major* he uses parodies of the extravagant style of Hippias, and I have not softened these in English. Hippias is given to rhyme and repetition ("most often and on the most"—281b2); redundancy ("unreasonably and unobservantly and foolishly and uncomprehendingly"—301c2–3); and ostentatiously balanced antithesis (as at 281c2–3). Compare these passages with the speech from Plato's *Protagoras* 337c7–338b1.

HIPPIAS
MAJOR

Socrates. Here comes Hippias, fine and wise! How long　281a
it's been since you put in to Athens!

Hippias. No spare time, Socrates. Whenever Elis[1] has
business to work out with another city, they always come first
to me when they choose an ambassador. They think I'm the
citizen best able to judge and report messages from the various　281b
cities. I've often been on missions to other cities, but most often
and on the most and greatest affairs to Sparta. That, to answer
your question, is why I don't exactly haunt these parts.

S. That is what it is like to be truly wise, Hippias, a man of
complete accomplishments: in private you are able to make a
lot of money from young people (and to give still greater
benefits to those from whom you take it); while in public you
are able to provide your own city with good service (as is　281c
proper for one who expects not to be despised, but admired by
ordinary people).

But Hippias, how in the world do you explain this: in the
old days people who are still famous for wisdom—Pittacus and
Bias and the school of Thales of Miletus, and later ones down
to Anaxagoras—that all or most of those people, we see, kept
away from affairs of state?[2]

H. What do you think, Socrates? Isn't it that they were
weak and unable to carry their good sense successfully into　281d
both areas, the public and the private?

S. Then it's really like the improvements in other skills,
isn't it, where early craftsmen are worthless compared to
modern ones? Should we say that your skill—the skill of the
sophists—has been improved in the same way, and that the
ancients are worthless compared to you in wisdom?

H. Yes, certainly, you're right.

S. So if Bias came to life again in our time, Hippias,
he would make himself a laughingstock compared with you　282a

53

people, just as Daedalus[3] also, according to the sculptors, would be laughable if he turned up now doing things like the ones that made him famous.

H. That's right, Socrates, just as you say. However *I* usually praise the ancients who came before us before and more highly than I praise people of our own day, for while I take care to avoid the envy of the living, I fear the wrath of the dead.

282b

S. You're putting fine thoughts in fine words, Hippias; that's what I think. I can support the truth of your claim; the skill you people have has really been improved in its ability to handle public business as well as private.

Why, Gorgias of Leontini,[4] the well-known sophist, came here on public business as ambassador from his home-town—because he was best qualified in Leontini to handle community affairs. In the assembly, he won his case, and in private, by giving displays and tutorials to young people, he

282c

made a lot of money and took it out of the city. Or, another case, our colleague Prodicus[5] came often enough on public business; but just this last time, when he came on public business from Ceos, he made a great impression with his speech in the council, and in private he earned a wonderful sum of money giving displays and tutoring the young. But none of these early thinkers thought fit to charge a monetary fee or give

282d

displays of his wisdom for all comers. They were so simple they didn't realize the great value of money. But either Gorgias or Prodicus made more money out of wisdom than any other craftsman made from any skill whatever. And Protagoras[6] did the same even earlier.

H. Socrates, you haven't the slightest idea how fine this can be. If you knew how much money *I've* made, you'd be

282e

amazed. Take one case: I went to Sicily once, when Protagoras was visiting there (he was famous then, and an older man); though I was younger I made much more than a hundred and fifty minas in a short time—and from one very small place, Inycum, more than twenty minas. When I went home with this I gave it to my father, so that he and the other citizens were amazed and thunderstruck. And I almost think I've made more money than any other two sophists you like put together.

S. That's a fine thing you say, Hippias, strong evidence

283a

of your own and modern wisdom, and of the superiority of men nowadays over the ancients. There was a lot of ignorance

among our predecessors down to Anaxagoras, according to
you. People say the opposite of what happened to you
happened to Anaxagoras: he inherited a large sum, but lost
everything through neglect—there was so little *intelligence*[7] in
his wisdom. And they tell stories like that about other early
wise men. You make me see there's fine evidence, here, I think,
for the superiority of our contemporaries over those who came 283b
before; and many will have the same opinion, that a wise man
needs to be wise primarily for his own sake. The mark of being
wise, I see, is when someone makes the most money. Enough
said about that.

Tell me this: from which of the cities you visit did you
make the most money? From Sparta, obviously, where you
visited most often.

H. Lord no, Socrates.

S. Really? Did you make the least?

H. Nothing at all, ever.   283c

S. That's weird, Hippias, and amazing! Tell me, isn't the
wisdom you have the sort that makes those who study and
learn it stronger in virtue?

H. Very much so, Socrates.

S. But while you were able to make the sons of Inycans
better, you were powerless for the sons of Spartans?

H. Far from it.

S. But then do Sicilians want to become better, but not
Spartans?

H. Certainly the Spartans want to, as well, Socrates. 283d

S. Well, did they stay away from you for lack of money?

H. No. They have enough.

S. How could it be that they have money and the desire,
and you have the ability to give them the greatest benefits, but
they didn't send you away loaded with money? Could it be this,
that the Spartans educate their own children better than you
would? Should we say this is so, do you agree?

H. Not at all.   283e

S. Then weren't you able to persuade the young men in
Sparta that if they studied with you they would make more
progress in virtue than if they stayed with their own teachers?
Or couldn't you persuade their fathers they should entrust the
matter to you, rather than look after it themselves, if they cared
at all for their sons? Surely they didn't enviously begrudge their
own sons the chance to become as good as possible.

H. I don't think they begrudged it.

S. But Sparta really is law-abiding.[8]

H. Of course.

284a   *S.* And what's most highly prized in law-abiding cities is virtue.

H. Of course.

S. And you, you know most finely of men how to pass virtue on to other people.

H. Very much so, Socrates.

S. Well, a man who knew most finely how to teach skill with horses would be most honored, and get the most money, in Thessaly, or wherever else in Greece that skill is seriously studied.

H. That's likely.

284b   *S.* Then won't a man who can teach lessons of the greatest value for virtue be given the highest honor, and make the most money, if he wishes, in Sparta, or in any other law-abiding Greek city? But you think it will be more in Sicily, more in Inycum? Should we believe all this, Hippias? If *you* give the order, it has to be believed.

H. An ancestral tradition of the Spartans, Socrates, forbids them to change their laws, or to give their sons any education contrary to established customs.

284c   *S.* What do you mean? The Spartans have an ancestral tradition of not doing right, but doing wrong?

H. I wouldn't say so, Socrates.

S. But they would do right to educate their young men better, not worse?

H. Right, indeed. But foreign education is not lawful for them: because, mind you, if anybody else had ever taken money from there for education, I would have taken by far the most—they love my lectures and applaud—but, as I say, it's against the law.

284d   *S.* Do you call law harmful or beneficial to the city, Hippias?

H. I think it is made to be beneficial, but sometimes it does harm, too, if the law is made badly.

S. But look here. Don't lawmakers make law to be the greatest good to the city? Without that, law-abiding civilized life is impossible.

H. True.

S. So when people who are trying to make laws fail to

make them good, they have failed to make them lawful—
indeed, to make them law. What do you say?

H. In precise speech, Socrates, that is so. But men are not   284e
accustomed to use words in that manner.

S. Do you mean those who know, Hippias, or those who
don't?

H. Ordinary people.

S. Are *they* the ones who know the truth—ordinary
people?

H. Of course not.

S. But I suppose people who know, at least, believe that
what is more beneficial is more lawful in truth for all men. Do
you agree?

H. Yes, I grant it's that way in truth.

S. Then it is and stays just the way those who know believe
it to be?

H. Quite.

S. But, as you say, it would be more beneficial for the
Spartans to be educated by your teaching, though it's foreign—   285a
more beneficial than the local education?

H. And what I say is true.

S. And that what is more beneficial is more lawful—do
you say that too, Hippias?

H. I did say it.

S. By your account it is more lawful for the sons of the
Spartans to be educated by Hippias and less lawful by their
fathers, if they will really be more benefited by you.

H. They certainly will be benefited, Socrates.   285b

S. Then the Spartans are breaking the law by not giving
you money and entrusting their sons to you.

H. I grant that. I think you said your say on my behalf, and
there's no need for me to oppose it.

S. So we find the Spartans to be lawbreakers, and that on
the most important issue, though they appear to be most
lawful. So when they applaud you, really, Hippias, and enjoy
your speech, what sort of things have they heard? Surely
they're those things you know most finely, things about stars   285c
and movements in the sky?

H. Not at all. They can't stand the subject.

S. Then do you enjoy hearing about geometry?

H. No. Many of them can't even, well, *count*.

S. Then they're a long way from putting up with your

displays of arithmetic.

H. Good god, yes. A long way.

S. Well, do they like those things on which you know how
285d   to make the sharpest distinctions of anybody—the functions
of letters, syllables, rhythms, and harmonies?

H. Harmonies and letters, indeed!

S. Well just what is it they love to hear about from you,
and applaud? Tell me yourself; I can't figure it out.

H. The genealogies of heroes and men, Socrates, and the
settlements (how cities were founded in ancient times), and in a
285e   word all ancient history—that's what they most love to hear
about. So because of them I have been forced to learn up on all
such things and to study them thoroughly.

S. Good lord, Hippias, you're lucky the Spartans don't
enjoy it when someone lists our archons from the time of
Solon.[9] Otherwise, you'd have had a job learning them.

H. How come, Socrates? Let me hear them once and I'll
memorize fifty names.

S. That's right. I forgot you had the art of memory. So I
286a   understand: the Spartans enjoy you, predictably, because you
know a lot of things, and they use you the way children use old
ladies, to tell stories for pleasure.

H. Yes—and, good lord, actually about fine activities,
Socrates. Just now I made a great impression there speaking
about the activities a young man should take up. I have a
speech about that I put together really finely, and I put the
words particularly well. My setting and the starting-point of
the speech are something like this: After Troy was taken, the
286b   tale is told that Neoptolemus asked Nestor[10] what sort of
activities are fine—the sort of activities that would make
someone most famous if he adopted them while young. After
that the speaker is Nestor, who teaches him a very great many
very fine customs. I displayed that there and I expect to display
it here the day after tomorrow, in Pheidostratus' schoolroom—
with many other fine things worth hearing. Eudicus,[11] Apē-
286c   mantus' son, invited me. But why don't you come too, and
bring some more people, if they are capable of hearing and
judging what is said?

S. Certainly, Hippias, if all goes well. But now answer me
a short question about that; it's a fine thing you reminded me.
Just now someone got me badly stuck when I was finding fault
with parts of some speeches for being foul, and praising other

parts as fine. He questioned me this way, really insultingly: "Socrates, how do *you* know what sorts of things are fine and foul? Look, would you be able to say what the fine is?"[12] And I, I'm so worthless, I was stuck and I wasn't able to answer him properly. As I left the gathering I was angry and blamed myself, and I made a threatening resolve, that whomever of you wise men I met *first,* I would listen and learn and study, then return to the questioner and fight the argument back. So, as I say, it's a fine thing you came now. Teach me enough about what the fine is itself, and try to answer me with the greatest precision possible, so I won't be a laughingstock again for having been refuted a second time. Of course you know it clearly; it would be a pretty small bit of learning out of the many things *you* know. 286d

286e

H. Small indeed, Socrates, and not worth a thing, as they say.

S. Then I'll learn it easily, and no one will ever refute me again.

H. No one will. Or what I do would be crude and amateurish. 287a

S. Very well said, Hippias—*if* we defeat the man! Will it hurt if I act like him and take the other side of the argument when you answer, so that you'll give me the most practice? I have some experience of the other side. So if it's the same to you I'd like to take the other side, to learn more strongly.

H. Take the other side. And, as I just said, the question is not large. I could teach you to answer much harder things than that so no human being could refute you. 287b

S. That's amazingly well said! Now, since it's your command, let me become the man as best I can and try to question you. If you displayed that speech to him, the one you mentioned about the fine activities, he'd listen, and when you stopped speaking he'd ask not about anything else but about the fine—that's a sort of habit with him—and he'd say: "O visitor from Elis, is it not by justice[13] that just people are just?" Answer, Hippias, as if *he* were the questioner. 287c

H. I shall answer that it is by justice.

S. "And is this justice *something?*"

H. Very much so.

S. "And by wisdom wise people are wise, and by the good all good things are good?"

H. How could they be otherwise?

S. "... by these each *being* something? Of course, it can't be that they're not."

H. They are.

S. "Then all fine things, too, are fine by the fine, isn't that so?"

287d

H. Yes, by the fine.

S. "... by that being *something?*"

H. It is. Why not?

S. "Tell me then, visitor," he'll say, "what is that, the fine?"

H. Doesn't the person who asks this want to find out what is a fine thing?

S. I don't think so, Hippias. What is *the* fine.

H. And what's the difference between the one and the other?

S. You don't think there is any?

H. There's no difference.

S. Well, clearly your knowledge is finer. But look here,

287e   he's asking you not what is a fine thing, but what is the fine.

H. My friend, I understand. I will indeed tell him what the fine is, and never will I be refuted. Listen, Socrates, to tell the truth, a fine girl is a fine thing.

S. That's fine, Hippias; by Dog[14] you have a glorious answer. So you really think, if *I* gave that answer, I'd be

288a   answering what was asked, and correctly, and never will I be refuted?

H. Socrates, how could you be refuted when you say what everyone thinks, when everyone who hears you will testify that you're right?

S. Very well. Certainly. Now, look, Hippias, let me go over what you said for myself. *He* will question me somewhat like this: "Come now, Socrates, give me an answer. All those things you say are fine, will they be fine if the fine itself is *what?*" Shall I say that if a fine girl is a fine thing, those things will be fine because of that?

288b

H. Then do you think that man will still try to refute you—that what you say is not a fine thing—or if he does try, he won't be a laughingstock?

S. You're wonderful! But I'm sure he'll try. Whether trying will make him a laughingstock—we'll see about that. But I want to tell you what he'll say.

H. Tell me.

S. "How sweet you are, Socrates," he'll say. "Isn't a fine

Elean mare a fine thing? The god praised mares in his oracle.''   288c
What shall we say, Hippias? Mustn't we say that the mare is a
fine thing? At least if it's a fine one. How could we dare deny
that the fine thing is a fine thing?

  H. That's true, Socrates. And the god was right to say that
too. We breed very fine mares in our country.

  S. "Very well," he'll say. "What about a fine lyre? Isn't it a
fine thing?" Shouldn't we say so, Hippias?

  H. Yes.

  S. Then after that he'll ask—I know fairly well, judging
from the way he is—"Then what about a fine pot, my good
fellow? Isn't it a fine thing?"

  H. Who is the man, Socrates? What a boor he is to dare   288d
in an august proceeding to speak such vulgar speech that way!

  S. He's like that, Hippias, not refined. He's garbage, he
cares about nothing but the truth. Still the man must have an
answer; so here's my first opinion: *If* the pot should have been
turned by a good potter, smooth and round and finely fired,
like some of those fine two-handled pots that hold six choes,
very fine ones—*if* he's asking about a pot like that, we have   288e
to agree it's fine. How could we say that what is fine is not
a fine thing?

  H. We couldn't, Socrates.

  S. "Then is a fine pot a fine thing too? Answer me!" he'll
say.

  H. But I think that's so, Socrates. Even that utensil is fine
if finely made. But on the whole that's not worth judging fine,
compared to a horse and a girl and all the other fine things.

  S. Very well. Then I understand how we'll have to answer   289a
him when he asks this question, here: "Don't you know that
what Heracleitus said holds good—'the finest of monkeys is
foul put together with another[15] class,' and the finest of pots is
foul put together with the class of girls, so says Hippias the
wise." Isn't that so, Hippias?

  H. Of course, Socrates. Your answer's right.

  S. Then listen. I'm sure of what he'll say next. "What?
If you put the class of girls together with the class of gods,   289b
won't the same thing happen as happened when the class of
pots was put together with that of girls? Won't the finest girl be
seen to be foul? And didn't Heracleitus (whom you bring in)
say the same thing too, that 'the wisest of men is seen to be a
monkey compared to god in wisdom and fineness and

everything else?'" Should we agree, Hippias, that the finest girl is foul compared to the class of gods?

H. Who would object to that, Socrates?

289c   *S.* Then if we agreed to that, he'd laugh and say, "Socrates, do you remember what you were asked?" "Yes," I'll say: "Whatever is the fine itself?" "Then," he'll say, "when you were asked for the fine, do you answer with something that turns out to be no more fine than foul, as you say yourself?" "Apparently," I'll say. Or what do you advise me to say, my friend?

H. That's what I'd say. Because compared to gods, anyway, the human race is not fine—that's true.

289d   *S.* He'll say: "If I had asked you from the beginning what is both fine and foul, and you had given me the answer you just gave, then wouldn't you have given the right answer? Do you *still* think that the fine itself by which everything else is beautified and seen to be fine when that form[16] is added to it—that *that* is a girl or a horse or a lyre?"

H. But if *that's* what he's looking for, it's the easiest thing in the world to answer him and tell him what the fine (thing) is by which everything else is beautified and is seen to be fine when it is added. The man's quite simple; he has no feeling at all for fine possessions. If you answer him that this thing he's asking for, the fine, is just *gold,* he'll be stuck and won't try to refute you. Because we all know, don't we, that wherever that is added, even if it was seen to be foul before, it will be seen to be fine when it has been beautified with gold.

S. You have no experience of this man, Hippias. He stops at nothing, and he never accepts anything easily.

290a   *H.* So what? He *must* accept what's said correctly, or, if not, be a laughingstock.

S. Well, *that* answer he certainly will not accept, my friend. And what's more, he'll jeer at me, and say, "Are you crazy? Do you think Pheidias[17] is a bad workman?" And I think I'll say, "No, not at all."

H. And you'll be right about that.

S. Right enough. Then when I agree that Pheidias is a good workman, this person will say, "Next, do you think Pheidias didn't know about this fine thing you mention?" "What's the point?" I'll say. "The point is," he'll say, "that Pheidias didn't make Athena's eyes out of gold, nor the rest of her face, nor her feet, nor her hands—as he would have done if gold would really have made them be seen to be finest—but he made them out of ivory. Apparently he went wrong through ignorance; he didn't know gold was what made everything fine, wherever it is added." What shall we answer when he says that, Hippias?

H. It's not hard. We'll say he made the statue right. Ivory's fine too, I think. 290c

S. "Then why didn't he work the middles of the eyes out of ivory? He used stone, and he found stone that resembled ivory as closely as possible. Isn't a stone a fine thing too, if it's a fine one?" Shall we agree?

H. Yes, at least when it's appropriate.

S. "But when it's not appropriate it's foul?" Do I agree or not?

H. Yes, when it's not appropriate anyway.

S. "Well," he'll say. "You're a wise man! Don't ivory and gold make things be seen to be fine when they're appropriate, but foul when they're not?" Shall we be negative? Or shall we agree with him that he's right? 290d

H. We'll agree to *this:* whatever is appropriate to each thing makes that particular thing fine.

S. "Then," he'll say, "when someone boils the pot we just mentioned, the fine one, full of fine bean soup, is a gold stirring spoon or a figwood one more appropriate?"

H. Herakles! What kind of man is this! Won't you tell me who he is? 290e

S. You wouldn't know him if I told you the name.

H. But I know right now he's an ignoramus.

S. Oh, he's a real plague, Hippias. Still, what shall we say? Which of the two spoons is appropriate to the soup and the pot? Isn't it clearly the wooden one? It makes the soup smell better, and at the same time, my friend, it won't break our pot, spill out the soup, put out the fire, and make us do without a truly noble meal, when we were going to have a banquet. That gold spoon would do all these things; so *I* think we should say the figwood spoon is more appropriate than the gold one, unless you say otherwise. 291a

H. Yes, it's more appropriate. But *I* wouldn't talk with a man who asked things like that.

S. Right you are. It wouldn't be appropriate for you to be filled up with words like that, when you're so finely dressed, finely shod, and famous for wisdom all over Greece. But it's nothing much for me to mix with him. So help me get prepared. 291b

Answer for my sake. "If the figwood is really more appropriate than the gold," the man will say, "wouldn't it be finer? Since you agreed, Socrates, that the appropriate is finer than the not appropriate?"

Hippias, don't we agree that the figwood spoon is finer than the gold one?

H. Would you like me to tell you what you can say the fine is—and save yourself a lot of argument?

291c *S.* Certainly. But not before you tell me how to answer. Which of those two spoons I just mentioned is appropriate and finer?

H. Answer, if you'd like, that it's the one made of fig.

S. Now tell me what you were going to say. Because by *that* answer, if I say the fine is gold, apparently I'll be made to see that gold is no finer than wood from a figtree. So what do you say the fine is this time?

291d *H.* I'll tell you. I think you're looking for an answer that says the fine is the sort of thing that will never be seen to be foul for anyone, anywhere, at any time.

S. Quite right, Hippias. Now you've got a fine grasp of it.

H. Listen now, if anyone has anything to say against *this,* you can certainly say I'm not an expert on anything.

S. Tell me quickly, for god's sake.

H. I say, then, that it is always finest, both for every man and in every place, to be rich, healthy, and honored by the 291e Greeks, to arrive at old age, to make a fine memorial to his parents when they die, and to have a fine, grand burial from his own children.

S. Hurray, Hippias! What a wonderful long speech, worthy of yourself! I'm really delighted at the kind way in which—to the best of your ability—you've helped me out. But we didn't hit the enemy, and now he'll certainly laugh at us harder than ever.

H. That laughter won't do him any good, Socrates. When he has nothing to say in reply, but laughs anyway, he'll be 292a laughing at himself, and he'll be a laughingstock to those around.

S. That may be so. But maybe, as I suspect, he'll do more than laugh at me for that answer.

H. What do you mean?

S. If he happens to have a stick, and I don't run and run away from him, he'll try to give me a thrashing.

H. What? Is the man your owner or something? Do you mean he could do that and not be arrested and convicted? Or don't you have any laws in this city, but people are allowed to hit each other without any right? 292b

S. No, that's not allowed at all.

H. Then he'll be punished for hitting you without any right.

S. I don't think so, Hippias. No, if I gave *that* answer he'd have a right—in *my* opinion anyway.

H. Then I think so too, seeing that you yourself believe it.

S. Should I tell you why *I* believe he'd have a right to hit me if I gave that answer? Or will you hit me without trial too? Will you hear my case?

H. It would be awful if I wouldn't. What do you have to say? 292c

S. I'll tell you the same way as before. I'll be acting out his part—so the words I use are not directed against you; they're like what he says to me, harsh and grotesque. "Tell me, Socrates," you can be sure he'll say, "do you think it's wrong for a man to be whipped when he sings such a dithyramb[18] as that, so raucously, way out of tune with the question?" "How?" I'll say. "How!" he'll say. "Aren't you capable of remembering that I asked for the fine itself? For what when added to any- 292d thing—whether to a stone or a plank or a man or a god or any action or any lesson—*anything* gets to be fine? I'm asking you to tell me what fineness is itself, my man, and I am no more able to make you hear me than if you were sitting here in stone—and a millstone at that, with no ears and no brain!"

Hippias, wouldn't you be upset if I got scared and came back with this: "But that's what Hippias said the fine was. And 292e I asked him the way you asked me, for that which is fine always and for everyone." So what do you say? Wouldn't you be upset if I said that?

H. Socrates, I know perfectly well that what I said is fine for everyone—everyone will think so.

S. "And *will* be fine?" he'll ask. "I suppose the fine is always fine."

H. Certainly.

S. "Then it *was* fine, too," he'll say.

H. It was.

S. "For Achilles as well?" he'll ask. "Does the visitor from Elis say it is fine for *him* to be buried after his parents? And for

293a   his grandfather Aeacus? And for the other children of the gods? And for the gods themselves?"[19]

    H. What's that? Go to blessedness. These questions the man asks, Socrates, they're sacrilegious!

    S. What? Is it a sacrilege to say that's so when someone else asks the question?

    H. Maybe.

    S. "Then maybe you're the one who says that it is fine for everyone, always, to be buried by his children, and to bury his parents? And isn't Herakles included in 'everyone' as well as everybody we mentioned a moment ago?"

    H. But I didn't mean it for the *gods*.

293b   *S*. "Apparently you didn't mean it for the heroes either."

    H. Not if they're children of gods.

    S. "But if they're not?"

    H. Certainly.

    S. "Then according to your latest theory, I see, what's awful and unholy and foul for some heroes—Tantalus and Dardanus and Zethus—is fine for Pelops and those with similar parentage."

    H. That's my opinion.

    S. "Then what you think is what you did not say a moment ago—that being buried by your children and burying your
293c parents is foul sometimes, and for some people. Apparently it's still more impossible for that to become and be fine for everyone; so that has met the same fate as the earlier ones, the girl and the pot, and a more laughable fate besides: it is fine for some, not fine for others. And to this very day, Socrates, you aren't able to answer the question about the fine, what it is."

    That's how he'll scold me—and he's right if I give him such an answer.

293d   Most of what he says to me is somewhat like that. But sometimes, as if he took pity on my inexperience and lack of education, he himself makes me a suggestion. He asks if I don't think such and such is the fine, or whatever else he happens to be investigating and the discussion is about.

    H. How do you mean?

    S. I'll show you. "You're a strange man, Socrates," he'll say, "giving answers like that, in that way. You should stop
293e that. They're very simple and easy to refute. But see if you think this sort of answer is fine. We had a grip on it just now when we replied that gold is fine for things it's appropriate to,

but not for those it's not. And anything else is fine if *this* has been added to it: this, the appropriate itself—the nature of the appropriate itself. See if it turns out to be the fine."

I'm used to agreeing with such things every time, because I don't know what to say. What do you think? Is the appropriate fine?

H. In every way, Socrates.

S. Let's look it over. We'd better not be deceived.

H. We have to look it over.

S. See here, then. What do we say about the appropriate: is it what makes—by coming to be present—each thing to which it is present *be seen to be fine,* or *be fine,* or neither?   294a

H. I think it's what makes things be seen to be fine. For example, when someone puts on clothes and shoes that suit him, even if he's ridiculous, he is seen to be finer.

S. Then if the appropriate makes things be seen to be finer than they are, it would be a kind of deceit about the fine, and it wouldn't be what we are looking for, would it, Hippias? I thought we were looking for that by which all fine things are   294b
fine. For example, what all large things are large by is *the projecting.* For by that all large things—even if they are not seen to be so—if they project they are necessarily large. Similarly, we say the fine is what all things are fine by, whether or not they are seen to be fine. What would it be? It wouldn't be the appropriate. Because that makes things be seen to be finer than they are—so you said—and it won't let things be seen to be as they are. We must try to say what it is that makes things   294c
fine, whether they are seen to be fine or not, just as I said a moment ago. That's what we're looking for, if we're really looking for the fine.

H. But Socrates, the appropriate makes things both be fine and be seen to be fine, when it's present.

S. Is it impossible for things that are really fine not to be seen to be fine, since what makes them be seen is present?

H. It's impossible.

S. Then shall we agree to this, Hippias: that everything really fine—customs and activities both—are both thought to   294d
be, and seen to be, fine always, by everybody? Or just the opposite, that they're unknown, and individuals in private and cities in public both have more strife and contention about them than anything?

H. Much more the latter, Socrates. They are unknown.

S. They wouldn't be, if "being seen to be" had been added to them. And that would have been added if the appropriate were fine and made things not only be but be seen to be fine. Therefore, if the appropriate is what makes things fine, it would be the fine we're looking for, but it would not be what makes things be seen to be fine. Or, if the appropriate is what makes things be seen to be fine, it wouldn't be the fine we're looking for. Because *that* makes things be; but by itself it could not make things be seen to be and be, nor could anything else. Let's choose whether we think the appropriate is what makes things be seen to be, or be, fine.

H. It's what makes things be seen to be, in my opinion, Socrates.

S. Oh dear! It's gone and escaped from us, our chance to know what the fine is, since the appropriate has been seen to be something other than fine.

H. God yes, Socrates. And I think that's very strange.

S. But we shouldn't let it go yet, my friend. I still have some hope that the fine will make itself be seen for what it is.

H. Of course it will. It's not hard to find. I'm sure if I went off and looked for it by myself—in quiet—I would tell it to you more precisely than any preciseness.

S. Ah, Hippias! Don't talk big. You see how much trouble it has given us already; and if it gets mad at us I'm afraid it will run away still harder. But that's nonsense. You'll easily find it, I think, when you're alone. But for god's sake, find it in front of me, or look for it with me if you want, as we've been doing. If we find it, that would be the finest thing; but if not, I will content myself with my fate, while you go away and find it easily. And if we find it now, of course I won't be a nuisance to you later, trying to figure out what it was you found on your own. Now see what you think the fine is: I'm saying that it's— pay attention now, be careful I'm not raving—let this be fine for us: whatever is useful. What I had in mind when I said that was this. We say eyes are fine not when we think they are in such a state they're unable to see, but whenever they *are able,* and are useful for seeing. Yes?

H. Yes.

S. And that's how we call the whole body fine, sometimes for running, sometimes for wrestling. And the same goes for all animals—a fine horse, rooster, or quail—and all utensils and means of transport on land and sea, boats and warships,

294e

295a

295b

295c

295d

and the tools of every skill, music and all the others; and, if you want, activities and laws—virtually all these are called fine in the same way. In each case we look at the nature it's got, its manufacture, its condition; then we call what is useful "fine" in respect of *the way* it is useful, *what* it is useful *for,* and *when* it   295e
is useful; but anything useless in all those respects we call "foul." Don't you think that way too, Hippias?

H. Yes, I do.

S. So then are we right to say now that the useful more than anything turns out to be fine?

H. Right, Socrates.

S. So what's *able* to accomplish a particular thing is useful for that for which it is able; and what's unable is useless.

H. Certainly.

S. Then is ability fine, but inability foul?

H. Very much so. Many things give us evidence for the   296a
truth of that, especially politics. The finest thing of all is to be able politically in your own city, and to be unable is the foulest of all.

S. Good! Then doesn't it follow from these points that, by god, wisdom is really the finest thing of all, and ignorance the foulest?

H. What are you thinking?

S. Keep quiet, my friend. I'm frightened. What on earth are we saying now?

H. Why should you be frightened now? The discussion   296b
has gone really well for you this time.

S. I wish it had! Look this over with me: could anyone do something he doesn't know how to do, and isn't at all able to do?

H. Not at all. How could he do what he isn't able to do?

S. Then when people make mistakes, do bad work, even when they do it unintentionally—if they aren't able to do things, they wouldn't ever do them, would they?

H. That's clear.

S. But people who are able are able by ability? I don't   296c
suppose it's by inability.

H. Of course not.

S. And everyone who does things is able to do the things he does.

H. Yes.

S. And all men do much more bad work than good,

starting from childhood—and make mistakes unintentionally.

H. That's right.

S. So? We don't call that ability and that sort of useful
thing fine, do we? The sort that's useful for doing some
bad piece of work? Far from it.

H. Far indeed, Socrates. That's what I think.

S. Then this able and useful of ours is apparently not the
fine, Hippias.

H. It is, Socrates, if it's able to do good, if it's useful for
that sort of thing.

S. Then here's what got away from us: the able-and-useful
without qualification is fine. And this is what our mind wanted
to say, Hippias: the useful-and-able for making some good—
that is the fine.

H. I think so.

S. But that is beneficial. Isn't it?

H. Certainly.

S. Then that's the way fine bodies and fine customs and
wisdom and everything we mentioned a moment ago are
fine—because they're beneficial.

H. That's clear.

S. So the beneficial appears to be the fine we wanted.

H. Certainly, Socrates.

S. But the beneficial is the maker of good.

H. It is.

S. And the maker is nothing else but the cause, isn't it?

H. That's so.

S. Then the fine is a cause of the good.

H. It is.

S. But the cause is different from what it's a cause of. I
don't suppose the cause would be a cause of a cause.[20] Look at
it this way: isn't the cause seen to be a maker?

H. Certainly.

S. Then what is made by the maker is the thing that comes
to be; it's not the maker.

H. That's right.

S. Then the thing that comes to be and the maker are
different things.

H. Yes.

S. So the cause isn't a cause of a cause, but of the thing
that comes to be because of it.

H. Certainly.

S. So if the fine is a cause of the good, the good should come to be from the fine. And apparently this is why we're eager to have intelligence and all the other fine things: because their product, their child—the good—is worth being eager about. It would follow that the fine is a kind of father of the good.

H. Certainly. You're talking fine, Socrates.

S. Then see if this is fine as well: the father is not a son and the son is not a father.   297c

H. Fine.

S. The cause is not a thing that comes to be, and the thing that comes to be is not a cause.

H. That's true.

S. Good god! Then the fine is not good, nor the good fine. Or do you think they could be, from what we've said?

H. Good god, no. I don't think so.

S. So are we happy with that? Would you like to say that the fine is not good, nor the good fine?

H. Good god, no. I'm not at all happy with it.

S. Good god, yes, Hippias. Nothing we've said so far makes me less happy.   297d

H. So it seems.

S. Then it doesn't turn out to be the finest account, as we thought a moment ago, that the beneficial—the useful and the able for making some good—is fine. It's not that way at all, but if possible it's more laughable than the first accounts, when we thought the girl, or each one of those things mentioned earlier, was the fine.

H. Apparently.

S. And *I* don't know where to turn, Hippias. I'm stuck. Do you have anything to say?

H. Not at present; but as I said a little while ago, I'm sure   297e
I'll find it when I've looked.

S. But I don't think I can wait for you to do that, I have such a desire to know. And besides I think I just got clear. Look. If whatever makes us be glad, not with all the pleasures, but just through hearing and sight—if we call *that* fine, how do you suppose we'd do in the contest?[21]

Men, when they're fine anyway—and everything decora-   298a
tive, pictures and sculptures—these all delight us when we see them, if they're fine. Fine sounds and music altogether, and speeches and storytelling have the same effect. So if we

answered that tough man, "Your honor, the fine is what is pleasant through hearing and sight," don't you think we'd curb his toughness?

H. This time, Socrates, I think what the fine is has been well said.

298b   *S.* What? Shall we say that fine activities and laws are fine by being pleasant through hearing and sight? Or that they have some other form?

H. Those things might slip right past the man.

S. By Dog, Hippias, not past the person I'd be most ashamed to babble at, or pretend to say something when I'm not saying anything.

H. Who's that?

S. Sophroniscus' son.[22] He wouldn't easily let me say those

298c   things without testing them, any more than he'd let me talk as if I knew what I didn't know.

H. Well for my part, since you say so, I think that's something else in the case of the laws.

S. Keep quiet, Hippias. We could well be thinking we're in the clear again, when we've gotten stuck on the same point about the fine as we did a moment ago.

H. What do you mean, Socrates?

S. I'll show you what's become obvious to me, if I'm saying

298d   anything. In the case of laws and activities, those could easily be seen not to be outside the perception we have through hearing and sight. But let's stay with this account, that what is pleasing through them is fine, and not bring that about the laws into the center. But if someone should ask—whether he's the one I mentioned or anyone else—"What, Hippias and Socrates? Are you marking off the sort of pleasant you call fine from the

298e   pleasant, and not calling what is pleasant to the other senses fine—food and drink, what goes with making love, and all the rest of that sort of thing? Aren't they pleasant? Do you say there's altogether no pleasure in such things? Not in anything but seeing and hearing?"

What shall we say, Hippias?

H. Of course we'll say there are very great pleasures in those others, Socrates.

S. "What?" he'll say. "Though they're no less pleasures than these, would you strip them of this word, and deprive

299a   them of being fine?"

"Yes," we'll say, "because anyone in the world would

laugh at us if we called it not *pleasant to eat* but *fine,* or if we called a pleasant smell not *pleasant* but *fine.* And as for making love, everybody would fight us; they'd say it is most pleasant, but that one should do it, if he does it at all, where no one will see, because it is the foulest thing to be seen." When we've said that, Hippias, he'd probably reply, "I understand that too. You're ashamed, you've been ashamed a long time, to call those pleasures fine, because men don't think they are. But I didn't ask for that—what ordinary people think is fine—but for what *is* fine."

299b

I think we'll repeat our hypothesis: "This is what we say is fine, the part of the pleasant that comes by sight and hearing." What else would you do with the argument? What should we say, Hippias?

H. We must say that and nothing else, in view of what's been said.

S. "That's fine," he'll say. "Then if the pleasant through sight and hearing is fine, whatever is not pleasant in that way clearly would not be fine."

299c

Shall we agree?

H. Yes.

S. "Then is the pleasant through sight pleasant through sight and hearing? Or is the pleasant through hearing pleasant through hearing and through sight?"

"By no means," we'll say. "In that case what comes through one would be what comes through both—I think that's what you mean—but *we* said that each of these pleasant things taken itself by itself is fine, and both are fine as well."

Isn't that our answer?

H. Certainly.

299d

S. "Then," he'll say, "does one pleasant thing differ from another in *this:* in being pleasant? I'm not asking whether one pleasure can be greater or lesser than another, or more or less, but whether one can differ in this very way—in being a pleasure—and one of the pleasures not be a pleasure."

We don't think so, do we?

H. We don't think so.

S. "So," he'll say. "You selected those pleasures from the other pleasures because of something different from their being pleasures. You saw some quality in the pair of them, something that differentiates them from the others, and you say they are fine by looking at that. I don't suppose pleasure through sight

299e

is fine because of *that*—that it is through sight. Because if that were the cause of its being fine, the other—the one through hearing—wouldn't ever be fine. It's not a pleasure through sight."

That's true. Shall we say that's true?

H. We'll say it.

300a   *S.* "And again, pleasure through hearing turns out not to be fine because of *that*—that it is through hearing. Otherwise, pleasure through sight would never be fine, because it is not a pleasure through hearing."

Shall we say that the man who says this is saying the truth, Hippias?

H. It's true.

S. "But both are fine, as you say." We do say that.

H. We do.

S. "Then they have some thing that itself makes them be fine, that common thing that belongs to both of them in

300b   common and to each privately. Because I don't suppose there's any other way they would both and each be fine."

Answer me as you would him.

H. I think it's as he says, and that's my answer.

S. Then if something is attributed to both pleasures but not to each one, they would not be fine by that attribute.

H. And how could that be, Socrates? That when neither has an attribute, whatever it may be, this attribute—which belongs to neither—could belong to both?

300c   *S.* Don't you think it could happen?

H. If it did I'd be in the grip of a lot of inexperience about the nature of these things and the terms of the present terminology.

S. Pleasantly put, Hippias. But maybe I'm turning out to think I can see something that's the way you say it can't be, or I'm not seeing anything.

H. It turns out that you're not, Socrates. You're quite readily mis-seeing.

S. And yet a lot of things like that are seen plainly in my mind; but I don't believe them if they're not imagined in yours,

300d   since you're a man who's made the most money by wisdom of anyone alive, and I'm one who never made anything. And I wonder, my friend, if you're not playing with me and deliberately fooling me, so many and so clear are the examples I see.

H. Socrates, no one will know finer than you whether

I'm playing or not, if you try to say what these things are that are seen by you plainly. You'll be seen to be saying nothing. Because never shall you find what is attributed to neither me nor you, but is attributed to both of us.

S. What do you mean, Hippias? Maybe you're saying   300e
something I don't understand. But listen more clearly to what I want to say. Because I see what is not attributed to me to be, and what neither I am nor you are, and this can be attributed to both of us. And there are others besides, which are attributed to both of us to be, things neither of us is.

H. Your answers seem weird again, Socrates, more so than the ones you gave a little earlier. Look. If both of us were just, wouldn't each of us be too? Or if each of us were unjust, wouldn't both of us? Or if we were healthy, wouldn't each be?   301a
Or if each of us had some sickness or were wounded or stricken or had any other tribulation, again, wouldn't both of us have that attribute? Similarly, if we happened to be gold or silver or ivory, or, if you like, noble or wise or honored or even old or young or anything you like that goes with human beings, isn't it really necessary that each of us be that as well?

S. Of course.   301b

H. But Socrates, *you* don't look at the entireties of things, nor do the people you're used to talking with. You people knock away at the fine and the other beings by taking each separately and cutting it up with words. Because of that you don't realize how great they are—naturally continuous bodies of being. And now you're so far from realizing it that you think there's some attribute or being that is true of these both but not   301c
of each, or of each but not of both. That's how unreasonably and unobservantly and foolishly and uncomprehendingly you operate.

S. That's the way things are for us, Hippias. "They're not the way a person wants"—so runs the proverb people often quote—"but the way he can get them." But your frequent admonitions are a help to us. This time, for example, before these admonitions from you about the stupid way we operate . . . Shall I make a still greater display, and tell you what we had in mind about them? Or not tell?   301d

H. You're telling someone who already knows, Socrates. I know how everybody who's involved in speeches operates. All the same, if it's more pleasant for you, speak on.

S. It really is more pleasant. We were so foolish, my friend, before you said what you did, that we had an opinion about me and you that *each* of us is *one,* but that we wouldn't *both* be *one* (which is what *each* of us would be) because we're not *one* but

301e *two*—we were so stupid-like. But now, we have been instructed by you that if two is what we both are, two is what each of us must be as well; and if each is one, then both must be one as well. The continuous theory of *being,* according to Hippias, does not allow it to be otherwise; but whatever both are, that each is as well; and whatever each is, both are. Right now I sit here persuaded by you. First, however, remind me, Hippias. Are you and I one? Or are you two and I two?

H. What do you mean, Socrates?

S. Just what I say. I'm afraid of you, afraid to speak

302a clearly, because you get angry at me whenever you think you've said anything. All the same, tell me more. Isn't each of us one, and *that*—being one—is attributed to him?

H. Certainly.

S. Then if each of us is one, wouldn't he also be odd-numbered? Or don't you consider *one* to be odd?

H. I do.

S. Then will both of us be odd-numbered, being two?

H. It couldn't be, Socrates.

S. But both are even-numbered. Yes?

H. Certainly.

S. Then because both are even-numbered, on account of *that,* each of us is even-numbered as well. Right?

302b *H.* Of course not.

S. Then it's not entirely necessary, as you said it was a moment ago, that whatever is true of both is also true of each, and that whatever is true of each is also true of both.

H. Not that sort of thing, but the sort I said earlier.

S. They're enough, Hippias. We have to accept them too, because we see that some are this way, and others are not this way. I said (if you remember how this discussion got started) that pleasure through sight and hearing was not fine by

302c *this*—that each of them turned out to have an attribute but not both, or that both had it but not each—but by that by which both and each are fine, because you agreed that they are both and each fine. That's why I thought it was by the being that adheres to both, if both are fine—it was by *that* they had to be fine, and not by what falls off one or the other. And I still think so now. But let's make a fresh start. Tell me, if the pleasure

through sight and the one through hearing are both and each   302d
fine, doesn't what makes them fine adhere in both and in each
of them?

H. Certainly.

S. Then is it because each and both are *pleasure*—would
they be fine because of that? Or would that make all other
pleasures no less fine than these? Remember, we saw that they
were no less pleasures.

H. I remember.

S. But is it because they are through sight and hearing—
are they called *fine* because of that?   302e

H. That's the way it was put.

S. See if this is true. It was said, I'm remembering, that
the pleasant was fine this way: not all the pleasant, but
whatever is through sight and hearing.

H. True.

S. Doesn't that attribute adhere in both, but not in each? I
don't suppose each of them is through both (as we said earlier),
but both through both, not each. Is that right?

H. Yes.

S. Then *that's* not what makes each of them fine; it doesn't
adhere in each (because "both" doesn't adhere in each). So the
hypothesis lets us call both of them fine, but it doesn't let us call
each of them fine.

What else should we say? Isn't it necessarily so?   303a

H. So we see.

S. Then should we call both fine, but not call each fine?

H. What's to stop us?

S. *This* stops us, friend, in my opinion. We had things that
come to belong to particular things in this way: if they come to
belong to both, they do to each also; and if to each, to both—all
the examples you gave. Right?

H. Yes.

S. But the examples *I* gave were not that way. Among them
were "each" itself and "both." Is that right?

H. It is.

S. With which of these do you put the fine, Hippias? With   303b
those you mentioned? If I am strong and so are you, we're both
strong too; and if I am just and so are you, we both are too. And
if both, then each. In the same way, if I am fine and so are you,
we both are too; and if both, then each. Or does nothing
stop them from being like the things I said I saw clearly: when   (303c)

both of anything are even-numbered, each may be either odd-
or possibly even-numbered. And again, when each of them is
inexpressible, both together may be expressible, or possibly
303c   inexpressible.[23] And millions of things like that. With which do
you place the fine? Do you see the matter the way I do? I think
it's a great absurdity for both of us to be fine, but each not; or
each fine, but both not, or anything else like that.

Do you choose the way I do, or the other way?

H. The first way is for me, Socrates.

303d   *S.* Well done, Hippias! We've saved ourselves a longer
search. Because if the fine is with *those,* then the pleasant
through sight and hearing is not fine anymore. "Through sight
and hearing" makes both fine, but not each. But that's
impossible, as you and I agree, Hippias.

H. We do agree.

S. Then it's impossible for the pleasant through sight and
hearing to be fine, since if it becomes fine it presents one of the
impossibilities.

H. That's right.

S. "Tell me again from the beginning," he'll say; "since you
303e   were quite wrong with that. What do you say that is—the fine
in both pleasures, which made you value them above the others
and call them fine?" Hippias, I think we have to say that they
are the most harmless pleasures and the best, both and each as
well. Or can you mention something else that distinguishes
them from all the others?

H. Not at all. They really are best.

S. He'll say, "Then this is what you say is the fine—
beneficial pleasure?"

"Apparently so," I'll say. And you?

H. Me too.

S. He'll say: "The maker of good is beneficial, but we just
saw that the maker and what is made are different. Your
304a   account comes down to the earlier account. The good would
not be fine, nor the fine good, if each of these were different."

"Absolutely," we'll say, if we have any sense. It's not
proper to disagree with a man when he's right.

H. But Socrates, really, what do you think of all that? It's
flakings and clippings of speeches, as I told you before, divided
up small. But here's what is fine and worth a lot: to be able to
304b   present a speech well and finely, in court or council or any other
authority to whom you give the speech, to convince them and

go home carrying not the smallest but the greatest of prizes, the successful defense of yourself, your property, and friends. One should stick to that.

He should give up and abandon all that small-talking, so he won't be thought a complete fool for applying himself, as he is now, to babbling nonsense.[24]

S. Hippias, my friend, you're a lucky man, because you know which activities a man should practice, and you've practiced them too—successfully, as you say. But I'm apparently held back by my crazy luck. I wander around and I'm always getting stuck. If I make a display of how stuck I am to you wise men, I get mud-spattered by your speeches when I display it. You all say what you just said, that I am spending my time on things that are silly and small and worthless. But when I'm convinced by you and say what you say, that it's much the most excellent thing to be able to present a speech well and finely, and get things done in court or any other gathering, I hear every insult from that man (among others around here) who has always been refuting me. He happens to be a close relative of mine, and he lives in the same house. So when I go home to my own place and he hears me saying those things, he asks if I'm not ashamed that I dare discuss fine activities when I've been so plainly refuted about the fine, and it's clear I don't even know at all what *that* is itself![25] "Look," he'll say. "How will you know whose speech—or any other action—is finely presented or not, when you are ignorant of the fine? And when you're in a state like that, do you think it's any better for you to live than die?" That's what I get, as I said. Insults and blame from you, insults from him. But I suppose it is necessary to bear all that. It wouldn't be strange if it were good for me. I actually think, Hippias, that associating with both of you has done me good. The proverb says, "What's fine is hard"—I think I know *that*.

304c

304d

304e

Footnotes to the *HIPPIAS MAJOR*

1. Elis was a city-state in the northwest Peloponnesus, not far from Olympia. The city-states of Greece were independent sovereign powers. At the time of this conversation, Athens and Sparta were vying for leadership of these city-states through alliances and conquest. Although geographically close to Sparta, Elis was tilting toward Athens.

2. Pittacus ruled in Mytilene for ten years, about 600 B.C., and was famous as a lawgiver; Bias was a statesman of Priene, active in the mid sixth century B.C.; and Thales is said to have predicted the eclipse of 585 B.C. All three were included in the "Seven Sages." Anaxagoras (c.500–c.428) was a philosopher in whom Socrates in his youth had taken special interest (*Phaedo* 97c).

3. Daedalus was praised in legend as an inventor of lifelike statues for King Minos of Crete.

4. Gorgias (c. 483–376 B.C.) was a sophist and an innovative public speaker. On his teaching, see Plato's *Gorgias* 449a–461b and the opening of the *Meno,* with *Meno* 95c.

5. Prodicus of Ceos was a sophist who was contemporary with Socrates. For a parody of his style, see Plato's *Protagoras* 315d and 337a–c.

6. Protagoras (c. 490–c. 420) was probably the first sophist to charge a fee (*Protagoras* 349a) and certainly one of the most successful (*Meno* 91d). He taught his students the skills and virtues required for success in public office and private life (Protagoras 318e). His famous statement about knowledge ("man is the measure of all things") is discussed by Plato in the *Theaetetus* at 152a and following.

7. "Intelligence" (*nous*) was said to be prominent in Anaxagoras' philosophy as the source of order for the entire universe. This was the feature of his teaching that attracted Socrates (*Phaedo* 97b).

8. Sparta's severe laws and rigorous educational system were famous

80

throughout Greece, and made it a cliché that she was the most law-abiding city of Greece.

9. The chief elected magistrates of Athens were called archons. Solon was a lawgiver, political reformer, and poet (c. 640/635 to soon after 561/560 B.C.).

10. Neoptolemus, son of Achilles, is the type of the young hero; Nestor, the oldest of the Greeks around Troy, is the standard wise old man.

11. Eudicus was probably Hippias' host in Athens (*Hippias Minor* 363b). Nothing is known about Pheidostratus.

12. "The fine" (*to kalon*) has a variety of uses in commendation. The Greek word may be translated "beautiful," "admirable," "noble," "lovely," or "good." Here, for clarity, I adhere to one translation, "fine."

13. ". . . is it not by justice that just people are just": cf. *Euthyphro* 6d11 and *Phaedo* 100d7. Socrates means that if just people are just because they satisfy the definition of *justice,* it must be possible to define *justice.*

14. "by Dog" is a favorite oath of Socrates'.

15. Heracleitus, fragment 22B82 in Hermann Diels, *Die Fragmente der Vorsokratiker,* 6th ed. rev. Walther Kranz, Berlin: Weidmann, 1952. Here I translate what the manuscripts read, "another." The quotation at 289b5 is listed by Diels-Kranz as 22B83.

16. The fine is an example of what Plato calls a "form" (*eidos* or *idea*). See *Euthyphro* 6d. Later, Plato developed a metaphysical theory of Forms. See the discussions in the works by Woodruff, Allen, and Rist cited in the bibliography (p. 46).

17. Pheidias, (b. about 490 B.C.), an Athenian sculptor, was best known as designer of the Parthenon sculptures. The statue of Athena mentioned in the next paragraph was fashioned of ivory and gold for the Parthenon.

18. A dithyramb is a sort of choral ode heavily embellished with music. Plato distrusted such poetry (*Phaedrus* 238d).

19. Achilles' mother, Thetis, was immortal. His grandfather, Aeacus, was a son of the immortal god Zeus. Herakles, Tantalus, Dardanus, and Zethus were all said to be sons of Zeus. Pelops, son of Tantalus, was of human parentage.

20. Understand this to mean: you can be the cause of something whether or

not that something is a cause in its own right. For example, a father is the cause of his son whether or not the son grows up to be a father himself. Not every son is a father, and not every thing that *has* a cause *is* a cause. Take the rest of the argument in the same way: the fine could be the cause of good whether or not the good is itself fine. The definition does not require that the good be fine. But Socrates thinks it should.

21. On this proposal, see the interesting parallels at *Gorgias* 474d, ff., *Philebus* 51a, ff., and Aristotle, *Topics*, 146a21, ff.

22. Socrates is Sophroniscus' son.

23. By "inexpressible number" is probably meant an irrational surd (square root of a non-square number). The claim is false on the face of it. The sum of two such numbers is irrational. Scholars are divided on how to understand this passage. See Woodruff (1982), p. 87 n. 187.

24. See above, 301b2–301c3. *Gorgias* 486c provides an interesting parallel. See also *Hippias Minor* 369b8–369c8.

25. See above, 286c5–d2. Socrates apparently believes that you must know what the fine is before you can use the word "fine" correctly. This has been called a fallacy. See P.T. Geach, "Plato's *Euthyphro:* An Analysis and Commentary," *Monist,* 50 (1960), 369–382, Repr. in his *Logic that Matters* (Oxford, 1972), pp. 31–44, M.F. Burnyeat, "Examples in Epistemology: Socrates, Theaetetus and G.E. Moore," *Philosophy,* 52 (1977), 381–98, and the discussion in Woodruff (1982), pp. 138–141.

General Index

Able, the, 68–70 (295c–296d)
Achilles, 27 (535b), 38n18, 38n22, 65 (292e), 82n19
Aeacus, 66 (293a), 82n19
Aeschylus, 37n17
Aesthetics, 42
Allegorical interpretation, 36n2
Anaxagoras, 36n2, 53 (281c), 81n2, 81n7
Andromache, 27 (535b), 38n18
Antilochus, 29 (537a)
Antisthenes, 10
Apollodorus, 34 (541c), 39n25
Appropriate (*prepon*), 63 (290d, 291a), 64 (291b), 66–67 (293de); the appropriate as definition of the fine, 67–68 (294c–294e)
Archilochus, 6, 22 (531a), 23 (532a), 36n4
Archons, 58 (285e), 82n9
Arithmetic, 23 (531d), 58 (285c)
Art, 17
Asklepius, 21 (530a), 36n1
Athena, statue of, 62 (290b), 82n17
Athens, 34 (541cd), 39n26, 81n1, 82n9
Authenticity: of the *Ion*, 5; of the *Hippias Major*, 41

Bacchus, 37n14
Bacchus-worshippers, 26 (534a)
Barley-medicine, 30 (538c)
Beautiful. *See Kalos.*
Being, Hippias' theory of, 75 (301b), 76 (301e)

Beneficial, the, as definition of the fine, 70–71 (296e–297c), 78 (303e)
Bias, 53 (281cd), 81n2
Bodies of being, 75 (301b)
Both, *versus* Each, 73–78 (299c–303d)

Cause, 70–71 (296e–297c), 82n20
Chariot driving, 29 (537a)
Cithara, 37n9
Comedy: in the *Ion*, 9; in the *Hippias Major*, 41
Corybantes, 25 (534a), 28 (536c), 37n13
Craft, 17. *See also* Mastery, Profession
Craftsmen, 17, 53 (281d)
Cybele, 37n13

Daedalus, 25 (535b), 37n8, 54 (282a), 81n3
Daimonioi, translation of, 38n23
Dancers, 28 (536a)
Dance-song, 26 (534c), 37n16
Dardanus, 66 (293b), 82n19
Date: of the *Ion*, 5; of the *Hippias Major*, 44
Definition, 43
Democritus, on inspiration, 8n
Demodocus, 7
Dithyramb, 26 (534c), 37n16, 65 (292c), 82n18
Divination, 8, 22 (531b, 538e), 36n5
Doctors, 29 (537c), 31 (538c)

83

Dunatos, translation of, 49

Each, *versus* Both, 73–78 (299c–303d)
Elis, 53 (281a), 81n1
Encomia, 26 (534c), 37n16
Enthusiasm, 25 (533e), 27 (535c)
Epeius, 25 (533b), 37n8
Ephesus, 5, 21 (530a), 34 (541d), 39n26
Epic: poets, 25 (533e); poetry, 27 (535b)
Epidaurus, 21 (530a), 36n1
Eudicus, 58 (286b), 82n11
Euripides, 25 (533d)

Figwood, 63 (290d)
Fine, the (*to kalon*), 43, 44, 59 (286d), 60 (287cd), 71 (297c), 79 (304d), 82n12, 82n16, 83n25. *See also* Kalos
Fisherman, 31 (538d)
Forms: theory of, 42, 44, 82n16; bibliography, 46

Genealogies, 58 (285d)
Generals, as professionals, 33 (540d), 34 (541bc), 35 (541e)
Geometry, 57 (285c)
Gift, divine (*theia moira*), 26 (534c), 28 (536cd)
Girl, a, as definition of the fine, 60 (287e)
Glaucon, 21 (530d), 36n2
Goethe, 9
Gold, as definition of the fine, 62 (289e)
Good, the, 59 (287c), 71 (297c)
Gorgias, 54 (282b), 81n4

Hector, 27 (535b), 38n18, 39n24
Hecuba, 27 (535b), 38n18

Hekamede, 30 (538b)
Heracleia, 37n11
Heracleitus, 61 (289ab), 82n15
Herakleides, 34 (541d), 39n25
Herakles, 66 (293a), 82n19
Hermeneus, translation of, 17. *See also* Representatives
Hesiod, 6, 7, 22 (531a), 23 (532a), 36n4
Hippias profession of, 41, 42; style of, 49; ontology of, 75 (301bc), 76 (301e)
Homer, 6, 7, 10, 21 (530b, 530d), 22 (531a), 23 (531d), 24 (532b), 25 (533c), 28 (536b, 536de), 29 (537a), 30 (538b), 31 (538c), 34 (541b, 541e), 35 (542a), 36n2, 36n4, 38n18. *See also under* Index of Ancient Works
Hyporchēma (dance-song), 37n16

Iambic poetry, 26 (534c), 38n16
Inexpressible numbers (surds), 78 (303b), 83n23
Inspiration, 7–10, 25 (533e)
Intellect (*nous*), 26 (534bc)
Intelligence (*nous*), 55 (283a), 81n7
Interpretation: by rhapsodes, 6, 17; allegorical, 36n2
Inycum, 54 (282e)
Ion, the rhapsode, 5–7
Iris, 38n22
Iron rings, 25 (533d), 27 (535e)
Irrational numbers, 78 (303b), 83n23
Ivory, as definition for the fine, 63 (290c)

Justice, 59 (287c), 82n13

Kalos: translation, 17, 49;

discussed, 10, 42, 82n12, 83n25.
See also Fine, the
Knowledge, 7, 24 (532c), 29
(537de), 30 (538b), 34 (541e)

Laws, 56 (284d), 57 (284e), 72
(298b–d), 81n8
Literary criticism, 10
Lovely. See *Kalos*
Lyric: poets, 25 (533e); poems,
26 (534de)

Machaon, 30 (538c)
Madness, as inspiration, 8–9,
37n15
Magnesia, 37n11
Magnets, as image for inspiration,
25 (533d), 27 (535e), 37n11
Mastery, 24 (532c), 26 (534bc),
28 (536cd), 34 (541e) *See also*
Profession, *Technē*
Melampus, 38n23
Metrodorus, 6, 21 (530d), 36n2
Mimnermus, 6, 36n4
Musaeus, 28 (536b), 38n19
Muse, the, 7, 25 (533e), 26 (534b),
28 (536a), 37n12

Neoptolemus, 58 (286b), 82n10
Nestor, 29 (537a), 30 (538c), 58
(286b), 82n10
Nous. See Intellect, Intelligence

Odysseus, 27 (535b), 38n18
Olympus, legendary musician, 25
(533c), 37n10
Ontology: of Plato, 44; of
Hippias, 75 (301bc), 76 (301e)
Oracles, 9
Orpheus, 28 (536b), 37n10

Painting, 24 (532e)

Panathenaia, 36n1
Parthenon, 82n17
Patroclus, 29 (537a)
Pelops, 82n19
Phainesthai, translation of, 49
Phanosthenes, 34 (541d), 39n25
Pheidias, 62 (290a), 82n17
Pheidostratus, 58 (286b), 82n11
Phemius, 7, 25 (533c), 37n10
Phocylides, 6, 36n4
Pindar, 38n16. *See also under*
Index of Ancient Works
Pittacus, 53 (281c), 81n2
Plato: on inspiration, 7–8; on
poetry, 13; on definition, 45; on
beauty and the fine, 45
Pleasure, as definition of the fine,
71–73 (297e–299c), 76–78
(302c–303e)
Poetry, 24 (532c); poets, 7–10, 26
(534a–535a), 28 (536b), 37n15,
37n16
Polygnotus, 24 (532e), 37n7
Poseidon, 39n27
Possession, by muses, 26 (534a),
28 (536b–d)
Pot (*chytra*), 61 (288c)
Poulydamas, 38n24
Pramnos, 30 (538c), 38n21
Priam, 27 (535b), 38n18
Prodicus, 54 (282c), 81n5
Profession, 21 (530b), 29 (537c–e),
31 (538e), 32 (539e), 32 (540b).
See also Mastery, *Technē*
Prophecy, 8, 26 (534b)
Protagoras, 54 (282d), 81n6
Proteus, 34 (541e), 39n27
Pythia, 8–9

Representatives, poets as, 17, 26–
27 (534e–535a)
Rhapsodes, 5–6, 10, 17, 21 (530a),

24 (532d), 28 (536a), 30 (538b), 32 (539e), 34 (541b), 36n1, 36n4
Sculpture, 25 (533a)
Seven sages, 81n2
Skill, 17. *See also* Mastery, Profession
Small-talking, 79 (304b)
Socrates, 6–7, 42, 83n22; bibliography, 46; Socratic fallacy, 83n25, 59 (286cd), 79 (304d)
Solon, 58 (285e), 82n9
Sons of Homer, 22 (530d), 36n3
Sophists, 10, 42; bibliography, 46
Sophroniscus, 72 (298b), 83n22
Sparta, 34 (541c), 43, 53 (281b), 55 (283b), 56 (284b), 81n1, 81n8
Stesimbrotus, 6, 21 (530d), 36n2
Surds, 83n23

Tantalus, 66 (293b), 82n19
Technē: translation of, 17;

discussed, 7, 9–10; bibliography, 15. *See also* Mastery, Profession
Thales, 53 (281c), 81n2
Thamyrus, 25 (533c), 37n10
Theodorus, 25 (533b), 37n8
Theoklymenos, 31 (538e), 38n23
Thetis, 38n22, 82n19
Tynnichus, 26 (534d), 37n17

Useful, the, as definition of the fine, 69–70 (295e–296d)

Virtue, 55 (283c), 56 (284a)

Wisdom, 59 (287c)

Xenophon, 5, 6, 42. *See also under* Index of Ancient Works

Zethus, 66 (293b), 82n19

Index of Ancient Works

Aristophanes, *Birds* 748–51: 37n12

Aristotle, *Topics* 146a21: 83n21

Euripides, *Bacchae:* 37n14; *Oeneus:* 37n11

Hesiod, *Theogony* 31–34: 7

Homer, *Iliad:* 31 (539bd); *Il.* 11.639–40, 30 (530c), 38n21; *Il.* 12.200–207, 31–2 (539bd), 38n24; *Il.* 13.729–33, 39n24; *Il.* 20.80–82, 31 (538cd), 38n22; *Il.* 23.335–40, 29 (537ab), 38n20; *Odyssey:* 31 (538e), 32 (539d); *Od.* 8.62–3, 7; *Od.* 8.72–3, 7; *Od.* 20.351–57, 31 (539ab), 38n23; *Od.* 22.437–38, 7

Pindar: *Olympian* IX.26–7, 37n12; *Nemean* III.77–78, 37n14; *Paean* VI.6, 7

Plato: *Apology,* 42; *Ap* 22a–c, 6; *Euthyphro,* 44; *Eu.* 6d11, 82n13, 82n16; *Eu.* 15d, 39n27; *Gorgias* 463e–465d, 7; *Grg.* 474d, 83n21; *Grg.* 486c, 83n24; *Hippias Minor* 363b, 82n11; *HMn.* 369b8–c8, 83n24; *Ion* 534a, 8; *Laws* 719c, 8, 37n15; *Meno* 99cd, 6; *Phaedo,* 44; *Pd.* 97b, 81n2, 81n7; *Pd.* 100d7, 82n13; *Phaedrus* 238d, 82n18; *Pdr.* 245a, 8, 37n15; *Philebus* 51a, 83n21; *Republic,* 10; *Republic* 588d, 6; *Timaeus* 71e–72b, 8

Xenophon, *Symposium* iv.6–7, 38n20, 38n21